THE COOKIE JAR

THE COOKIE JAR

Over 90 scrumptious recipes
for home-baked treats

Liz Franklin
Photography by Kate Whitaker

RYLAND PETERS & SMALL
LONDON • NEW YORK

Designer Maria Lee-Warren
Senior Designer Megan Smith
Commissioning Editor Stephanie Milner
Production Manager Gordana Simakovic
Art Director Leslie Harrington
Editorial Director Julia Charles
Publisher Cindy Richards

Food Stylist Annie Rigg
Prop Stylist Jo Harris
Indexer Hilary Bird

First published in the UK and US in 2015.
This revised edition published in 2021
by Ryland Peters & Small
20–21 Jockey's Fields,
London WC1R 4BW
and
341 E 116th Street
New York, NY 10029

www.rylandpeters.com

10 9 8 7 6 5 4 3 2 1

Text copyright © Liz Franklin 2015, 2021
Design and photographs copyright ©
Ryland Peters & Small 2015, 2021

ISBN: 978-1-78879-239-4

Printed and bound in China

A CIP record for this book is available from
the British Library.

US Library of Congress Cataloging-in-
Publication Data has been applied for.

Notes

• Both British (metric) and American (imperial plus US cup) measurements are included in these recipes for your convenience, however it is important to work with one set of measurements only and not alternate between the two within a recipe.

• All spoon measurements are level unless otherwise specified.

• All eggs are medium (UK) or large (US), unless specified as large, in which case US extra-large should be used. Uncooked or partially cooked eggs should not be served to the very old, frail, young children, pregnant women or those with compromised immune systems. It is recommended that free-range, organic eggs be used whenever possible.

• Ovens should be preheated to the specified temperatures. We recommend using an oven thermometer. If using a fan-assisted oven, adjust temperatures according to the manufacturer's instructions.

• Whenever butter is called for within these recipes, salted butter should be used.

• When a recipe calls for the grated zest of citrus fruit, buy unwaxed fruit and wash well before using. If you can only find treated fruit, scrub well in warm soapy water before using.

CONTENTS

INTRODUCTION

There's something unquestionably magical about cookie baking. A simple dough goes into the oven and only minutes later you have golden, irresistible cookies that fill the whole kitchen with the most blissful aroma.

Most of us like a little sweet treat now and again, and making your own cookies at home makes that treat something really special, much nicer and far more gratifying than just blindly opening a packet of something you've picked up at the supermarket. And the best thing is that cookie doughs aren't generally difficult or time consuming to make, they don't need lots of complicated equipment – and both the dough and the cookies themselves tend to freeze really well, too!

Nowadays we are constantly told to cut down our intake of sugar, salt and snack foods – and that's no bad thing at all. But it doesn't mean we have to go without altogether. By making cookies at home rather than eating endless packets of store bought ones, we can control the amount of sugar and salt we add and avoid using hydrogenated fats that are so typical of the bought variety. Homemade cookies are more satisfying to eat too, and so it's less tempting to eat cookie after cookie... although I have to fess up to occasionally eating a few more than I should!

All of the cookies recipes that follow are made with ingredients that can be easily found in the supermarket. I always, always use real butter, or extra virgin olive oil in the crackers – never margarine. Margarines are often made from hydrogenated fats, and those that aren't are often a blend of various oils that leave a lot to be desired. I would rather have butter – which is a natural product with a lovely flavour – and eat less, which I find much easier to do with homemade goodies because they're far tastier and more fulfilling!

The selection of cookies I've included incorporates everything from simple to stylish and all of the cookies throughout can be packaged prettily and given as edible gifts. There are cookies to please all ages and for all occasions, from spooky Witches' fingers for Halloween to pretty lace-like tuiles to serve at the most elegant dinner party. There are cookies to comfort, biscuits to dunk and crisp crackers to top with crumbly cheese; favourites such as chocolate chip cookies, custard creams and buttery Scottish shortbread, as well as some that are a little less ordinary, such as chocolate-stuffed sablés, Garibaldi biscuits, delicate Florentines and fig rolls. Whether your preference is for something plain, or you're the original sweet-toothed Cookie Monster, I'm sure you'll find lots to delight as you work your way through the book. Happy cookie baking!

BASIC BAKING TIPS

Equipment

You may like to have some nice cookie cutters to hand, but apart from that, the usual mixing bowls and spoons and a couple of flat baking sheets are all that you will need. An electric handheld whisk helps for the recipes that involve stiffly beaten egg whites, and a food processor is a must for the macaron recipe on page 152, but most of the time I tend to avoid complicated cooking paraphernalia.

I like to line baking sheets with baking parchment rather than greaseproof paper as I find its non-stick properties more reliable. Non-stick silicone baking mats are really great too – they're made of fibreglass and food grade silicone and are available from specialist catering suppliers, cook shops and online. You simply wash them, roll them up and keep them in the cupboard to reuse time and time again.

I do collect cookie cutters, and there are lots of great suppliers on the high street and online. See Suppliers on page 11 and 192.

Ingredients

Poor ingredients will give poor results. All the recipes in this book are made with good-quality salted butter, or extra virgin olive oil. Please don't be tempted to substitute low fat margarines (or indeed any margarine), as the results just won't be the same.

Sometimes I read reviews of recipes (not just my own) where readers have substituted ingredients and changed this or that and they are not happy with the results. By all means experiment with flavours and such, but not by changing good-quality ingredients for inferior quality ingredients. If you do use unsalted butter, then it is important to add a pinch of salt to the recipe, as the flavour of the finished cookie will be a little flat without it.

Freezing the dough

Most of the cookies in this book are made from dough that freezes really well. The doughs that are rolled into log shapes can be wrapped tightly in clingfilm/plastic wrap and then in foil. Be sure to label them so that you know what you're getting when you take them back out again! When defrosting, if you give them a few minutes to thaw out, you can cut them into slices whilst they are still partially frozen and just add a few minutes on to the baking time. The cookies that are rolled into walnut-sized balls can be frozen in freezer-proof boxes, layered between baking parchment. You can cook them straight from the freezer, again adding a few minutes to the baking time. And the best bit is that you will always be able to have freshly baked cookies at your fingertips without too much trouble at all!

Storing cookies & crackers

All of the cookies and crackers in this book will need to be stored in an airtight container: a tin, sealed plastic box (such as Tupperware), Kilner type jar or a tight-lidded cookie jar.

Be careful when storing different types of cookies together, too – heavily spiced or highly flavoured cookies may taint any other type of cookie they are stored with and some types of softer or the more moist, chewier cookie can cause others to soften more quickly than they might if they were stored with drier, crisper biscuits. Delicate tuiles are best stored by themselves as they will soften easily and of course will break very quickly, too, but you are more likely to make a tuile for a specific serving purpose rather than as part of a mixture of cookies to keep in a cookie jar. Savoury crackers and biscuits are best stored separately from sweet cookies too, again to stop flavour transferral and premature softening.

Cooking times

All but a few of the recipes are cooked at 180°C (350°F) Gas 4. I'm all for making life easier to encourage people to cook at home rather than convincing themselves it's too much trouble! It's not easy to be very precise with cooking times, as that will be influenced directly by the size of cookie cutter that you have used. When a recipe calls for the dough to be rolled into walnut-sized balls, we might have differing ideas of the size of our walnuts too! Just keep an eye on the oven – none of the cookies will spoil if you take a peep and they're not quite done.

Suppliers

For some of the recipes in this book I have used specific cookie cutters. If you'd like to source the same shapes, sizes and types I recommend the following. For the Christmas tree stack on page 120, I use a set of star-shaped cookie cutters in descending sizes available from Lakeland and for 3-D effects, J B Cookie Cutters offer a wide range of standard and custom-made cutters that can be delivered worldwide. See page 192 for more of my favourite baking suppliers.

FOR ANY OCCASION

CHOC CHIP COOKIES

I haven't come across many people who can resist a freshly baked chewy chocolate-packed cookie – it's a bit like trying to say no to still-warm, straight-from-the-oven baked bread. One whiff of the heavenly smell coming from the oven alone, and self-restraint goes out of the window. For the best cookie, use good-quality chocolate chips – I like a mixture of dark/bittersweet and milk/semi-sweet chocolate, but you can stick to all or the other if you prefer. Sometimes I add a handful of halved, toasted hazelnuts and slightly less chocolate.

175 g/1 $^1/_2$ sticks butter, softened

80 g/scant $^1/_2$ cup soft brown sugar

80 g/scant $^1/_2$ cup caster/granulated sugar

1 egg

225 g/1 $^3/_4$ cups plain/all-purpose flour

$^1/_2$ teaspoon bicarbonate of soda/baking soda

100 g/$^2/_3$ cup milk/semi-sweet chocolate chips

100 g/$^2/_3$ cup dark/bittersweet chocolate chips

2 baking sheets lined with baking parchment

MAKES ABOUT 25

Preheat the oven to 180°C (350°F) Gas 4.

Put the butter and sugars together in a large mixing bowl and beat until light and fluffy. Add the egg and stir until fully incorporated. Mix the flour and bicarbonate of soda/baking soda together in a separate bowl and stir this into the cookie mixture. Add the chocolate chips and work everything together until evenly combined.

Roll the mixture into walnut-sized balls and arrange on the baking sheets, leaving a little space for spreading between each one.

Bake in the preheated oven for 8–10 minutes, until golden and firm.

Leave to cool for 5 minutes or so on the baking sheets, then transfer to a wire rack to cool completely. Store in an airtight container or cookie jar and eat within 5 days.

RUM & RAISIN COOKIES

The raisins in these cookies give them a lovely crisp-but-chewy texture, and the hint of rum just makes them even more special.

90 g/6 tablespoons butter, softened

175 g/^{3}/$_4$ cup plus 2 tablespoons Demerara/turbinado sugar

1 egg, lightly beaten

1 tablespoon rum

150 g/1 cup plus 2 tablespoons plain/all-purpose flour

50 g/^{1}/$_3$ cup dark raisins (or sultanas/golden raisins, if preferred)

2 baking sheets lined with baking parchment

MAKES ABOUT 20

Preheat the oven to 180°C (350°F) Gas 4.

Beat the butter and sugar together in a large mixing bowl until smooth. Add the egg and the rum. Stir in the flour and work everything together to form a smooth dough. Add the raisins and work gently into the dough until evenly incorporated.

Drop spoonfuls of the mixture onto the prepared baking sheets, leaving a little space for spreading between each one.

Bake in the preheated oven for 8–10 minutes, until golden and firm.

Leave to cool on the baking sheets, before transferring to a wire rack to cool completely. Store in an airtight container or cookie jar and eat within 1 week.

DOMINO BISCUITS

Decorated to look like real dominoes, these chocolatey biscuits are great fun for children and go down really well at birthday parties.

130 g/1 stick plus 1 tablespoon
butter

130 g/²/₃ cup caster/granulated
sugar

1 egg, beaten

200 g/1²/₃ cups plain/all-purpose
flour

60 g/¹/₃ cup ground almonds

20 g/2¹/₂ tablespoons
unsweetened cocoa powder

1 teaspoon baking powder

50 g/1¹/₂ oz. white chocolate,
melted

*2 baking sheets lined with
baking parchment*

MAKES ABOUT 30

Preheat the oven to 180°C (350°F) Gas 4.

Beat the butter and sugar together in a large mixing bowl until smooth. Add the egg, and continue to beat until fully incorporated. Stir in the flour, ground almonds, cocoa powder and baking powder, and bring the mixture together to form a stiff dough.

On a clean, lightly floured work surface, roll the dough out into a large rectangle with a thickness of about 3 mm/¹/₈ in. Cut out small rectangles just slightly larger than a real domino. Bring the trimmed dough (if there is any) together and roll out again to cut as many cookies out of the dough as possible.

Lay the cookies on the prepared baking sheets, leaving a little space for spreading between each one.

Bake in the preheated oven for 10–15 minutes, until firm.

Leave to cool on the baking sheets and then transfer to a wire rack to cool completely.

Use the melted white chocolate to decorate the biscuits with dots and lines to resemble dominoes. Store in an airtight container or cookie jar and eat within 1 week.

ICED COFFEE COOKIES

Coffee-flavoured glacé icing that sets ever-so-slightly crunchily makes these coffee cookies very moreish. A little sprinkling of very finely chopped walnuts around the outside perimeter give them an extra special touch, too – although you could use chocolate sprinkles or hazelnuts if you prefer.

150 g/1 stick plus 2 tablespoons butter, softened

120 g/²/₃ cup caster/superfine sugar

1 egg yolk

2 teaspoons instant coffee dissolved in 1 teaspoon boiling water

180 g/1¹/₃ cups plain/all-purpose flour

120 g/1 scant cup ground almonds

Coffee glaze

400 g/3²/₃ cups icing/confectioners' sugar

2 egg whites

2 teaspoons instant coffee dissolved in 1 teaspoon boiling water

100 g/²/₃ cup walnuts, very finely chopped

a round cookie cutter

2 baking sheets lined with baking parchment

MAKES 30

Preheat the oven to 180°C (350°F) Gas 4.

Beat the butter and sugar together in a large mixing bowl until smooth. Add the egg yolk and beat to combine. Stir in the coffee, and then add the flour and ground almonds and bring everything together to create a smooth dough.

On a clean, lightly floured work surface, roll out the dough into a large rectangle about 4 mm/¹/₈ in. thick. Cut out circles using the cookie cutter. Bring the trimmed dough together and roll out again to cut as many cookies out of the dough as possible.

Arrange the cookies on the prepared baking sheets and bake in the preheated oven for 8–10 minutes, until firm and golden.

Leave to cool on the baking sheet for about 5 minutes, before transferring to a wire rack to cool completely.

In the meantime, mix the icing/confectioners' sugar, egg whites and coffee together until smooth. Spread the coffee glaze over the cold cookies and sprinkle the chopped walnuts around the edges. Eat one, and then leave the rest until the glaze has set. Store in an airtight container or cookie jar between layers of baking parchment and eat within 3 days.

MALTESER COOKIES

I have to be honest here and say that I am not really sure of the exact weight of Maltesers/Whoppers that goes into these cookies. I always promise myself that I won't pick at them before they even get into the mixture, but I have yet to keep that particular promise. I also have a very annoying habit of eating the ones that sometimes drop out of the cookie dough, when the right thing to do would just be to push them back in again. Anyway, the exact measurement doesn't have to be too precise, I think, although the more Maltesers that end up in the dough, the better the cookie will be for sure!

80 g/5$^{1}/_{2}$ tablespoons butter, softened

130 g/$^{2}/_{3}$ cup soft brown sugar

1 egg, beaten

150 g/1 cup plus 2$^{1}/_{2}$ tablespoons plain/all-purpose flour

1 teaspoon baking powder

130 g/4$^{1}/_{2}$ oz. Maltesers/Whoppers

2 baking sheets lined with baking parchment

MAKES 18–20

Preheat the oven to 180°C (350°F) Gas 4.

Cream the butter and sugar together in a large mixing bowl until light and fluffy. Beat in the egg. Add the flour and baking powder, and bring the mixture together to form a soft dough.

Eat two of the Maltesers and then add the rest to the cookie dough. Take another two Maltesers from the packet to make up for the two you have just eaten and eat those as well to keep the weight as it is. Try to be good and push any strays that fall out of the mixture back in.

Drop spoonfuls of the cookie dough onto the prepared baking sheets, leaving a little space for spreading between each one.

Bake in the preheated oven for about 10 minutes, until the cookies are golden and firm.

Remove from the oven and leave to cool on the baking sheets for 10 minutes or so, before transferring to a wire rack to cool completely. Store in an airtight container or cookie jar and eat within 3 days.

left: stem ginger shortbread
right: gingernuts

STEM GINGER SHORTBREAD

Short and crumbly with a lovely zing of ginger, these are divine with a good cup of tea. Give the stem ginger a little rinse to get rid of the sticky syrup, and gently pat the nuggets dry on paper towels, or the residue syrup may add unwanted wetness to the dough and spoil the end result.

200 g/1²/₃ cups plain/all-purpose flour

160 g/1 stick plus 3 tablespoons butter, softened

70 g/³/₄ cup icing/confectioners' sugar

4–5 nuggets stem ginger, rinsed, dried and chopped

caster/superfine sugar, for dusting

a 4—5 mm/1 ³/₄—2 in. round cookie cutter

2 baking sheets lined with baking parchment

MAKES ABOUT 25

Preheat the oven to 180°C (350°F) Gas 4.

Put the flour, butter and icing/confectioners' sugar in a large mixing bowl and work together to form a smooth dough. Gently knead in the stem ginger.

On a clean, lightly floured work surface, roll the dough out into a large rectangle about 3–4 mm/¹/₈ in. thick. Cut out circles using the cookie cutter. Lay them on the prepared baking sheets, leaving a little space for spreading between each one. Bring the trimmed dough together and roll out again to cut as many cookies out of the dough as possible.

Bake in the preheated oven for 10–12 minutes, until firm and pale golden (the baking time will depend on the size of the cutter used).

Remove from the oven, dust with caster/superfine sugar and leave to cool for 5 minutes before transferring to a wire rack to cool completely. Store in an airtight container or cookie jar and eat within 1 week.

GINGERNUTS

I'm not sure why some ginger biscuits are called gingernuts, but I grew up with my mum having a serious addiction to them. Never a day would start until my mum had enjoyed a morning cuppa in bed, with two gingernuts alongside. If we had one, we were allowed to dunk ours in her tea (don't tell anyone I said that), because we weren't really that keen on having a full cup for ourselves. Anyway, these biccies are fabulous for anyone who is nuts about ginger... and that includes me. I've used spelt flour, which gives the cookies a chewy texture – ordinary plain/all-purpose flour will give a crunchier result. I use the crystallized ginger that is dry with a sugary coating, rather than stem ginger in syrup, and the exact amount is disputable too, because I can never resist munching on a piece or two as I'm cutting it up!

50 g/3^{1}/$_{2}$ tablespoons butter

100 g/^{3}/$_{4}$ cup spelt flour

50 g/^{1}/$_{4}$ cup Demerara/turbinado sugar

1 teaspoon ground ginger

1 teaspoon bicarbonate of soda/ baking soda

60 g/^{1}/$_{4}$ cup thick honey

80 g/^{1}/$_{2}$ cup crystallized ginger, chopped

a baking sheet lined with baking parchment

MAKES 12–15

Preheat the oven to 180°C (350°F) Gas 4.

Rub the butter and flour together in a large mixing bowl until it resembles fine breadcrumbs. Add the sugar, ginger and bicarbonate of soda/baking soda. Stir in the honey and then get your hands into the bowl and pull the mixture together into a soft dough. Add the crystallized ginger and work again, until it is evenly incorporated (although don't overwork the dough).

Form the mixture into 12–15 balls the size of small walnuts and lay on the prepared baking sheet, leaving a little space for spreading between each one. Flatten the balls lightly using the tines of a fork.

Bake in the preheated oven for about 10 minutes, until golden and firm.

Leave to cool on the baking sheet for 5 minutes or so, before transferring to a wire rack to cool completely. Store in an airtight container or cookie jar and eat within 1 week.

FIG ROLLS

Fig fans, these are for you. Don't be put off making them by the fact that they have a filling, buy the soft ready-to-eat figs and they're a doddle to make – and 100 per cent worth the effort anyway.

200 g/6^1/$_2$ oz. dried figs, coarsely chopped

2 teaspoons thick honey

150 g/1 cup plus 2^1/$_2$ tablespoons plain/all-purpose flour

100 g/1 cup ground almonds

80 g/^{1}/$_3$ cup plus 1 tablespoon caster/granulated sugar

150 g/1 stick plus 2 tablespoons butter, softened

2 egg yolks

a baking sheet lined with baking parchment

MAKES ABOUT 16

Preheat the oven to 180°C (350°F) Gas 4.

Put the figs and 200 ml/^{3}/$_4$ cups water into a saucepan and cook over a gentle heat until very soft. Add the honey and stir until the figs have fully broken down, or blitz with a handheld electric blender very briefly if preferred. Leave to cool.

Put the flour, ground almonds and sugar into a large mixing bowl and rub in the butter. Add 1 of the egg yolks and bring the mixture together with your hands to form a smooth dough.

Mix the other egg yolk with 1 tablespoon water to make an egg wash. Set aside.

Cut the dough into two equal pieces. On a clean, lightly floured work surface, roll out half of the dough into a long rectangle. Spoon half of the cooked fig mixture down one length of the dough, leaving a little space for sealing at the edge. Brush the edges with a little of the egg wash and fold the dough over as if you were making a sausage roll. Press the edges gently together to seal and cut into slices of about 3 cm/1^1/$_4$ in. Repeat with the remaining dough and filling.

Arrange the rolls on the prepared baking sheet and set aside.

Brush all the rolls with the egg wash and bake in the preheated oven for 15–20 minutes, until golden and firm.

Leave to cool on the baking sheet for 10–15 minutes, before transferring to a wire rack to cool completely. Store in an airtight container or cookie jar and eat within 3 days.

DOUBLE CHOC CHIP COOKIES

I don't know of many people who can resist a chewy chocolate chip cookie, and the fact that these are packed with both dark/bittersweet and milk/semi-sweet chocolate makes them even more tempting.

100 g/6$^{1}/_{2}$ tablespoons butter, softened

180 g/scant 1 cup dark muscovado sugar

50 g/$^{1}/_{4}$ cup caster/granulated sugar

a pinch of salt

1 egg

200 g/1$^{2}/_{3}$ cups plain/all-purpose flour

$^{1}/_{2}$ teaspoon bicarbonate of soda/ baking soda

100 g/$^{2}/_{3}$ cup dark/bittersweet chocolate chips

100 g/$^{2}/_{3}$ cup milk/semi-sweet chocolate chips

2 baking sheets lined with baking parchment

MAKES ABOUT 20

Preheat the oven to 180°C (350°F) Gas 4.

Beat the butter, muscovado sugar, caster/granulated sugar and salt together in a large mixing bowl until everything is well mixed. Add the egg, mix well and then add the plain/all-purpose flour and bicarbonate of soda/baking soda. Stir in the chocolate chips and bring the mixture together to form a soft dough.

Form the dough into balls the size of walnuts and place on the prepared baking sheets, leaving a little space for spreading between each one. Flatten the tops of the cookies slightly using the tines of a fork.

Bake in the preheated oven for 12–15 minutes, until the cookies are firm.

Transfer to a wire rack to cool, then store in an airtight container or cookie jar and eat within 5 days.

CRANBERRY & WHITE CHOC CHIP COOKIES

Chewy, fat cranberries are very slightly tart and go really well with white chocolate. Just make sure to look for really plump dried cranberries and use good-quality white chocolate. I use Lindt. Trust me, it makes a difference.

100 g/6½ tablespoons butter

150 g/³/₄ cup soft brown sugar

a pinch of salt

1 egg

220 g/1³/₄ cups self-raising/self-rising flour

100 g/1 cup dried cranberries

150 g/5 oz. white chocolate, chopped

2 baking sheets lined with baking parchment

MAKES ABOUT 20

Preheat the oven to 180°C (350°F) Gas 4.

Beat the butter, sugar and salt together in a large mixing bowl until everything is well mixed. Add the egg, mix well and then add the flour. Stir in the cranberries and chopped chocolate.

Form the dough into balls the size of walnuts and arrange on the prepared baking sheets, leaving a little space for spreading between each one. Flatten the tops of the cookies slightly by pressing gently with the tines of a fork.

Bake in the preheated oven for 12–15 minutes, until the cookies are firm.

Transfer to a wire rack to cool, and then store in an airtight container or cookie jar and eat within 5 days.

CHOCOLATE & VANILLA PINWHEELS

These delicious cookies not only look really pretty, but the contrast between the vanilla and chocolate doughs gives them a great flavour. They're always popular with young and old.

250 g/2 sticks butter

250 g/2 cups plain/all-purpose flour

a pinch of salt

seeds from 1 vanilla pod/bean (or $^1/_4$ teaspoon vanilla paste)

125 g/1 cup rice flour

125 g/$^2/_3$ cup caster/granulated sugar

20 g/2$^1/_2$ tablespoons unsweetened cocoa powder

2 baking sheets lined with baking parchment

MAKES ABOUT 40

Preheat the oven to 180°C (350°F) Gas 4.

Rub the butter, plain/all-purpose flour, salt, vanilla and rice flour together in a large mixing bowl until the mixture resembles fine breadcrumbs. Stir in the sugar and bring the mixture together to form a soft dough.

Divide the dough into two pieces, adding the cocoa powder to one. Lightly but firmly knead the dough until the cocoa powder is fully incorporated and has an even colour.

On a clean, lightly floured work surface, roll out both balls of dough into a large rectangle about 4 mm/$^1/_8$ in. thick. With the longest side facing towards you, place the chocolate dough over the top of the plain dough and roll the two together, as if you were making a Swiss roll/jelly roll, making sure to keep the two quite tight and the log evenly rolled.

Using a sharp knife, cut the dough into slices about 1 cm/$^3/_8$ in. thick and lay them on the prepared baking sheets.

Bake in the preheated oven for about 10 minutes, until firm and light golden.

Leave to cool on a wire rack and then store in an airtight container or cookie jar and eat within 1 week.

COCONUT FINGERS

50 g/3 1/2 tablespoons butter, softened

2 eggs, beaten

125 g/2/3 cup caster/granulated sugar

120 g/1 1/4 cups desiccated/shredded coconut

a pinch of salt

50 g/scant 1/2 cup plain/all-purpose flour

1/2 teaspoon bicarbonate of soda/baking soda

50 g/1 1/2 oz. dark/bittersweet chocolate, melted

a piping/pastry bag fitted with a large nozzle/tip

2 baking sheets lined with baking parchment

MAKES ABOUT 25

These are easy to make and always seem to be very popular with children at parties.

Preheat the oven to 180°C (350°F) Gas 4.

Beat the butter, eggs and sugar together in a large mixing bowl until smooth. Add the coconut, salt, flour and bicarbonate of soda/baking soda, and stir to combine.

Spoon the mixture into the piping/pastry bag and pipe finger shapes directly onto the prepared baking sheets, leaving a little space for spreading between each one.

Bake in the preheated oven for 8–10 minutes, until golden and firm.

Leave to cool on the baking sheets. Decorate with zigzags of melted chocolate across the length of the cookies and serve. Store in an airtight container or cookie jar and eat within 3 days.

CINNAMON SABLÉS

Anyone who loves cinnamon will find it hard to resist these lovely little biscuits with their lightly spiced flavour and pretty, crisp edges coated in cinnamon sugar.

180 g/1 $\frac{1}{2}$ sticks butter

100 g/$\frac{3}{4}$ cup plus 1 tablespoon icing/confectioners' sugar

250 g/2 cups plain/all-purpose flour

2 $\frac{1}{2}$ teaspoons ground cinnamon

3 tablespoons caster/superfine sugar

1 egg white, lightly whipped

2 baking sheets lined with baking parchment

MAKES ABOUT 30

Preheat the oven to 180°C (350°F) Gas 4.

Beat the butter and icing/confectioners' sugar together in a large mixing bowl until light and fluffy. Add the flour and 2 teaspoons of the cinnamon and mix until you have a smooth, soft dough.

Form the mixture into a long sausage shape, with a diameter of about 3 cm/1 $\frac{1}{4}$ in. and wrap in clingfilm/plastic wrap. Refrigerate for 30 minutes or so, to firm up.

Mix the caster/superfine sugar and the remaining cinnamon together in a wide, shallow dish.

Unwrap the dough and brush with the whipped egg white. Roll in the cinnamon sugar. Cut into discs about 1 cm/$\frac{3}{8}$ in. thick and place on the baking sheets, leaving a little space for spreading between each one.

Bake in the preheated oven for 10–15 minutes, until firm and golden.

Cool on a wire rack, store in an airtight container or cookie jar and eat within 1 week.

CARAMELIZED HONEY & ALMOND SQUARES

These elegant, shiny, almond-covered squares are a favourite with many of my friends and family. The great thing is that they're so easy to make, which is just as well, as they disappear incredibly quickly!

90 g/6 tablespoons butter

50 g/$\frac{1}{3}$ cup icing/confectioners' sugar

1 egg yolk

150 g/1 cup plus 2$\frac{1}{2}$ tablespoons plain/all-purpose flour

Almond topping

60 g/$\frac{1}{2}$ stick butter

100 g/$\frac{1}{2}$ cup caster/granulated sugar

2 tablespoons honey

5–6 tablespoons toasted flaked/slivered almonds

a baking sheet and a sheet of baking parchment of a similar size

MAKES ABOUT 15

Preheat the oven to 180°C (350°F) Gas 4.

Beat the butter and icing/confectioners' sugar together in a large mixing bowl until smooth. Add the egg yolk and beat again. Stir in the flour and bring everything together until you have a soft dough.

Roll the dough out onto a sheet of baking parchment roughly the same size as your baking sheet, until it is about 3–4 mm/$\frac{1}{8}$ in. thick. Transfer the rolled dough and parchment to the baking sheet and set aside.

For the almond topping, melt the butter, sugar and honey together in a small saucepan set over a medium heat. Allow to bubble for 2–3 minutes, until light golden. Add the flaked/slivered almonds and stir well.

Spoon the almond mixture over the biscuit base and bake in the preheated oven for about 8 minutes, until golden all over.

Leave to cool on the baking sheet, and then cut into squares or rectangles while still slightly warm. Store in an airtight container or cookie jar and eat within 3 days.

GINGERBREAD MEN

175 g/1$\frac{1}{3}$ cups plain/all-purpose flour

50 g/3$\frac{1}{2}$ tablespoons butter, softened

50 g/$\frac{1}{4}$ cup soft brown sugar

$\frac{1}{2}$ teaspoon bicarbonate of soda/ baking soda

1 teaspoon ground ginger

$\frac{1}{2}$ teaspoon mixed spice/apple pie spice

2 tablespoons golden syrup/ light corn syrup

1 egg yolk

To decorate

300 g/2$\frac{3}{4}$ cups icing/ confectioners' sugar

food colouring gels

sweets, to decorate (optional)

2 baking sheets lined with baking parchment

a gingerbread man or gingerbread woman cutter

a disposable piping/pastry bag

MAKES ABOUT 15

Children always love making and decorating gingerbread men. You could pipe on little icing trousers or skirts and use sweets for buttons. If you prefer, you could use melted white chocolate for piping rather than sugar icing.

Preheat the oven to 180°C (350°F) Gas 4.

Put the flour into a large mixing bowl and rub in the butter until the mixture resembles fine breadcrumbs. Add the sugar and mix. Stir in the bicarbonate of soda/baking soda, ground ginger and mixed spice/apple pie spice. Add the golden syrup/light corn syrup and egg yolk and bring the mixture together to form a smooth dough.

On a clean, lightly floured work surface, roll the dough out into a large rectangle with a thickness of about 3 mm/$\frac{1}{8}$ in. Cut out gingerbread men or women using the cookie cutter. Bring the trimmed dough together and roll out again to cut as many cookies out of the dough as possible.

Arrange the cookies on the prepared baking sheets and bake in the preheated oven for about 10 minutes, until firm and golden.

Remove from the oven and leave for 10 minutes or so to cool, before transferring to a wire rack to cool completely.

Mix the icing/confectioners' sugar together with enough water to form a thick icing, and spoon it into the piping/pastry bag. Decorate the cookies to look like little people, adding sweets as desired. Store in an airtight container or cookie jar and eat within 1 week.

SESAME COOKIES

A crisp sesame-coated edge makes these sesame-speckled cookies twice as nice to eat and utterly irresistible.

125 g/1 stick butter

125 g/$^2/_3$ cup caster/granulated sugar

1 egg

250 g/2 cups plain/all-purpose flour

80 g/$^3/_4$ cup sesame seeds, toasted

2 tablespoons Demerara/ turbinado sugar

1 egg white, lightly beaten

2 baking sheets lined with baking parchment

MAKES ABOUT 30

Preheat the oven to 180°C (350°F) Gas 4.

Beat the butter and caster/granulated sugar together in a large mixing bowl until smooth. Add the egg and beat until fully incorporated. Stir in the flour and 50 g/$^1/_2$ cup of the sesame seeds, and bring the mixture together to form a soft dough.

Form the dough into two sausage shapes and wrap tightly in clingfilm/plastic wrap. Refrigerate for 30 minutes or so, to firm up.

Mix the remaining sesame seeds and the Demerara/turbinado sugar together in a wide, shallow dish.

Unwrap the dough and brush with the beaten egg white. Roll in the sesame seeds and Demerara/turbinado sugar. Cut into discs about 1 cm/$^3/_8$ in. thick and place on the baking sheets, leaving a little space for spreading between each one.

Bake in the preheated oven for about 10 minutes, until golden and firm. Leave to cool for 5 minutes or so, before transferring to a wire rack to cool completely. Store in an airtight container or cookie jar and eat within 1 week.

MUESLI COOKIES

I use the packets of mixed nuts and seeds with lots of pumpkin, linseeds, sesame seeds and sunflower seeds for these oaty cookies. They give them a lovely flavour.

100 g/6¹/₂ tablespoons butter

generous 1 tablespoon honey

125 g/²/₃ cup Demerara/ turbinado sugar

a pinch of salt

100 g/³/₄ cup self-raising/self- rising flour

1 teaspoon bicarbonate of soda/ baking soda

180 g/1¹/₄ cups porridge oats

50 g/¹/₃ cup mixed nuts and seeds

50 g/¹/₃ cup sultanas/golden raisins

2 baking sheets lined with baking parchment

MAKES 15–20

Preheat the oven to 180°C (350°F) Gas 4.

Slowly melt the butter, honey, sugar and salt together in a saucepan set over a gentle heat.

Put the flour, bicarbonate of soda/baking soda, porridge oats, nuts and seeds and sultanas/golden raisins into a large mixing bowl. Pour in the melted butter and honey mixture and stir in 2 tablespoons water.

Form the cookie mixture into balls the size of walnuts and arrange on the prepared baking sheets, leaving a little space for spreading between each one. Press down gently to flatten them slightly.

Bake in the preheated oven for 12–15 minutes, until the cookies are firm.

Transfer to a wire rack to cool, and then store in an airtight container or cookie jar and eat within 1 week.

BRANDY SNAPS

I don't know anyone who doesn't love a brandy snap, with its crunchy snap and toffee-like flavour. Sometimes I leave out the ginger as I have a couple of friends who hate the stuff, but the biscuits themselves are generally a big crowd pleaser. You'll need to work quickly when shaping them into the traditional cigar shape, but don't worry if the mixture hardens before you've managed to get them wrapped around the spoon handle – simply pop them back into the oven for a few seconds until the mixture softens and becomes pliable again. If you don't have a wooden spoon (doesn't everyone have a wooden spoon?!) then simply drape them over a rolling pin to make tuile shapes.

100 g/6^1/$_2$ tablespoons butter

100 g/^{1}/$_2$ cup caster/granulated sugar

100 g/6 tablespoons golden syrup/light corn syrup

100 g/^{3}/$_4$ cup plain/all-purpose flour

^{1}/$_2$ teaspoon ground ginger

2 teaspoons brandy

2 baking sheets lined with baking parchment

MAKES 12–15

Preheat the oven to 180°C (350°F) Gas 4.

Melt the butter, sugar and golden syrup together in a small saucepan set over a medium heat, making sure to let the sugar dissolve. Stir in the flour, ground ginger and brandy.

Drop teaspoons of the mixture onto the prepared baking sheets, leaving quite a large amount of room for spreading between each one, and bake in the preheated oven for 5–6 minutes, until golden.

Remove from the oven, allow to cool for 30 seconds and then wrap carefully around the handle of a wooden spoon. Be careful – the sugar will be hot!

Leave to cool completely before storing in an airtight container or cookie jar for up to 2 days.

CHOCOLATE SANDWICHES

Depending on the size of cutter used, this should make about 15 sandwiches. Try not to be too heavy-handed when re-rolling the trimmings.

225 g/1 stick plus 7 tablespoons butter, softened

160 g/1 cup plus 1 tablespoon icing/confectioners' sugar

250 g/2 cups plain/all-purpose flour

80 g/²/₃ cup unsweetened cocoa powder

a pinch of salt

¹/₄ teaspoon baking powder

50 g/1 ¹/₂ oz. white chocolate

100 g/scant ¹/₂ cup Nutella, or chocolate spread, for filling

a small and large cookie cutter

2 baking sheets lined with baking parchment

MAKES 12–15

Preheat the oven to 180°C (350°F) Gas 4.

Beat the butter and sugar together in a large mixing bowl until smooth. Add the flour, cocoa powder, salt and baking powder. Mix well and draw the mixture together to form a smooth dough.

Roll the mixture out between two sheets of baking parchment, and cut circles out using a cookie cutter. Lay them on the prepared baking sheets. Using a smaller cookie cutter, cut circles out of the centre of half of the cookies and remove the dough. Bring the trimmed dough together and roll out again to cut as many cookies out of the dough as possible, making sure you have an even number of whole cookies and cookies with holes in. Arrange on the baking sheets with the other cookies.

Bake in the preheated oven for about 10 minutes, until firm.

Remove from the oven and cool on a wire rack.

Melt the white chocolate in a heatproof bowl set over a pan of barely simmering water. Decorate the cookies with holes in with zigzags of melted white chocolate in different directions.

Spread the whole cookies with Nutella and top with the decorated cookies with holes in.

Set aside to set, store between layers of baking parchment in an airtight container or cookie jar and eat within 3 days.

LEMON POLENTA COOKIES

These crunchy little cookies are a real crowd pleaser. At home in Italy I make them with big fat Sorrento lemons, and serve them with lemon sorbet or homemade ice cream. As ever, use unwaxed lemons.

250 g/2 cups plain/all-purpose flour

125 g/1 cup fine polenta/stone-ground cornmeal

125 g/^{2}/$_3$ cup caster/granulated sugar

grated zest of 1 large lemon

250 g/2 sticks salted butter, softened

2 baking sheets lined with baking parchment

MAKES ABOUT 24

Put the dry ingredients and lemon zest into a large mixing bowl and give them a good stir to mix in the lemon zest thoroughly and evenly. Add the butter and use your hands to work the mixture into a smooth dough. It shouldn't be too much of a task if the butter was softened.

Lay a piece of clingfilm/plastic wrap on a clean work surface. Lightly dust it with flour. Divide the mixture into two and roll one piece into a sausage shape on the clingfilm/plastic wrap. The roll should be about 4 cm/1^3/$_4$ in. in diameter. Wrap it tightly and twist the ends. Repeat with the remaining dough, using a new piece of clingfilm/plastic wrap. Refrigerate for 30 minutes, until the dough has firmed up.

Preheat the oven to 180°C (350°F) Gas 4.

Cut each chilled log into even slices. Lay the slices on the prepared baking sheets and bake in the preheated oven for 8–10 minutes, until golden and firm.

Let cool for 5 minutes on the baking sheets before transferring to a wire rack to cool completely. Store in an airtight container or cookie jar and eat within 1 week.

COFFEE CREAM SANDWICHES

If you love coffee and you love cookies, the chances are these will become a firm favourite! Use any shape of cookie cutter you like, or simply cut them into squares if you prefer.

175 g/1¹⁄₂ sticks butter, softened

75 g/¹⁄₂ cup icing/confectioners' sugar

1 egg yolk

1 tablespoon instant coffee dissolved in 1 teaspoon boiling water

250 g/2 cups plain/all-purpose flour

caster/superfine sugar, to dust

Coffee buttercream

100 g/6¹⁄₂ tablespoons butter, softened

200 g/2 cups icing/confectioners' sugar

1 teaspoon instant coffee dissolved in 1 teaspoon boiling water

a pinch of salt

a cookie cutter (optional)

2 baking sheets lined with baking parchment

MAKES ABOUT 15

Preheat the oven to 180°C (350°F) Gas 4.

Cream the butter and icing/confectioners' sugar together in a large mixing bowl until light and fluffy. Stir in the egg yolk and coffee. Add the flour and work everything together until the mixture forms a smooth dough.

On a clean, lightly floured work surface, roll the dough out into a large rectangle with a thickness of about 3 mm/¹⁄₈ in. Stamp out shapes with your chosen cutter (or cut into squares). Bring the trimmed dough together (if there is any) and roll out again to cut as many cookies out of the dough as possible. Arrange the cookies on the prepared baking sheets, leaving a little space in between each.

Bake in the preheated oven for 8–10 minutes, until firm.

Remove from the oven and leave to cool for several minutes, before transferring to a wire rack to cool completely.

Meanwhile, make the coffee buttercream. Beat the butter, icing/confectioners' sugar, coffee and salt together until smooth and creamy.

When the coffee cookies are completely cold, sandwich them together with the coffee buttercream.

Dust with a little caster/superfine sugar before serving or store in an airtight container or cookie jar and eat within 3 days.

WALNUT CRUNCH BISCUITS

Walnuts are a superfood: very good for the brain, I have read. So I like to eat these cookies when I'm having a cuppa and doing the crossword.

120 g/1 stick butter, softened

160 g/1¼ cups plain/all-purpose
   flour

60 g/5 tablespoons caster/
   granulated sugar

a pinch of salt

50 g/⅓ cup chopped walnuts

caster/superfine sugar, for
   dusting

*a baking sheet lined with baking
parchment*

MAKES 20–24

Preheat the oven to 160°C (300°F) Gas 2.

Put the butter, flour, caster/granulated sugar and salt in a large mixing bowl and work together to form a smooth dough. Gently knead in the walnuts.

Form the mixture into a long sausage shape, with a diameter of about 3 cm/ 1¼ in. and wrap in clingfilm/plastic wrap. Refrigerate for 30 minutes or so, until firm.

Remove the clingfilm/plastic wrap and cut the dough into discs about 5 mm/ ³/₁₆ in. thick. Arrange on the prepared baking sheet, leaving space between each to allow for spreading.

Bake in the preheated oven for 15 minutes or so, until firm and golden.

Cool on a wire rack, dust with a little caster/superfine sugar, store in an airtight container or cookie jar and eat within 1 week.

PEANUT BUTTER COOKIES

It's really important to use good-quality, crunchy unsweetened peanut butter here, otherwise the cookies will be too sweet. These are lovely sandwiched together with a little raspberry jam/jelly – it recreates the flavours of the classic American combo peanut butter and jelly. They're great for people on a gluten-free diet and can be rustled up in next to no time. My lovely friend Rick goes bonkers about them.

300 g/1¼ cups unsweetened crunchy peanut butter

1–2 tablespoons soft brown sugar

a pinch of salt

2 eggs, beaten

50 g/⅓ cup roasted and salted peanuts, crushed

a baking sheet lined with baking parchment

MAKES ABOUT 10

Preheat the oven to 180°C (350°F) Gas 4.

Put the peanut butter into a large mixing bowl and stir in the sugar and salt. Add all but a tablespoon of the beaten eggs and mix thoroughly.

Form the mixture into balls the size of walnuts and arrange on the prepared baking sheets, leaving a little space for spreading between each one. Press down gently with the tines of a fork to flatten them slightly and glaze each one with the leftover beaten egg.

Bake in the preheated oven for 12–15 minutes, until the cookies are firm and golden.

Transfer to a wire rack to cool, store in an airtight container or cookie jar and eat within 1 week.

AROUND THE WORLD

BACI DI DAMA

The name baci di dama literally translate as 'ladies' kisses', a really enchanting name for a lovely little biscuit. I've filled them with an easy chocolate ganache, but if you're in a hurry you can cheat and use a good-quality chocolate spread, such as Nutella.

100 g/6$\frac{1}{2}$ tablespoons butter, softened

100 g/$\frac{1}{2}$ cup caster/granulated sugar

100 g/$\frac{2}{3}$ cup ground almonds

100 g/$\frac{3}{4}$ cup plain/all-purpose flour

Chocolate filling

50 g/1$\frac{1}{2}$ oz. dark/bittersweet chocolate, broken into pieces

20 g/4 teaspoons butter

a baking sheet lined with baking parchment

MAKES ABOUT 10

Preheat the oven to 180°C (350°F) Gas 4.

Beat the butter and sugar together in a large mixing bowl until the mixture is light and smooth. Add the ground almonds and flour and work the mixture together until you have a stiff dough.

Form the dough into balls about the size of small walnuts, and lay on the prepared baking sheet, leaving a little space for spreading between each one.

Bake in the preheated oven for about 10 minutes, until firm and golden.

Remove from the oven and leave to cool on a wire rack.

In the meantime, make the filling. Melt the chocolate in a bowl set over a saucepan of barely simmering water (or microwave on full power for one minute, stirring half way through). Remove the chocolate from the heat and beat in the butter. Leave to cool.

When the biscuits and the filling are completely cold, use the chocolate mixture to sandwich them together. Store in an airtight container or cookie jar (if there are any left!) and eat within 3 days.

SPECULOOS

Spelt flour gives these divine, lightly spiced cookies such a lovely chewy texture, and the smell that wafts from the oven as they are cooking makes me drool with the anticipation of that first bite of warm cookie. Of course they have to be checked and rechecked as they're cooling. I think that might mean I'm an addict...

100 g/6$^{1}/_{2}$ tablespoons butter,
  softened

60 g/$^{1}/_{4}$ cup set honey

150 g/$^{3}/_{4}$ cup Demerara/
  turbinado sugar

1 egg

250 g/2 cups spelt flour

1 teaspoon mixed spice/apple pie
  spice

1 teaspoon ground cinnamon

$^{1}/_{2}$ teaspoon bicarbonate of soda/
  baking soda

a 5 cm/2 in. round cookie cutter

*2 baking sheets lined with
  parchment paper*

MAKES 20–25

Preheat the oven to 180°C (350°F) Gas 4.

Beat the butter, sugar, honey and egg together in a large mixing bowl until smooth. Add the flour, spices and bicarbonate of soda/baking soda, and mix until you have a smooth stiff dough. Leave the dough to rest for 30 minutes.

On a clean, lightly floured work surface, roll the dough out into a large rectangle with a thickness of about 3 mm/$^{1}/_{8}$ in. Cut out circles using the cookie cutter. Bring the trimmed dough together and roll out again to cut as many cookies out of the dough as possible.

Arrange the cookies on the prepared baking sheets, leaving a little space for spreading between each one.

Bake in the preheated oven for 8–10 minutes, until firm and golden.

Leave to cool slightly before transferring to a wire rack to cool completely. Store in an airtight container or cookie jar and eat within 3 days.

LEMON & PISTACHIO CANTUCCINI

Free from saturated fats and full of flavour, these pretty, lemony little pistachio-flecked cantuccini are perfect to serve with coffee.

250 g/2 cups plain/all-purpose flour

160 g/³/₄ cup plus 1 tablespoon caster/granulated sugar

150 g/³/₄ cup ground almonds

150 g/1 cup shelled unsalted pistachio nuts

grated zest of 3 lemons, finely grated

3 eggs, beaten

a baking sheet lined with baking parchment

MAKES 20–25

Preheat the oven to 180°C (350°F) Gas 4.

Put the flour, sugar and ground almonds into a large mixing bowl. Mix together and add the pistachios. Stir in the lemon zest, add the beaten eggs and draw the mixture together to form a smooth dough.

On a clean, lightly floured work surface, gently knead the dough for a minute or two before forming the mixture into two logs.

Place the logs on the prepared baking sheet and bake in the preheated oven for about 30 minutes, until firm and golden. Remove from the oven, keeping the heat on, and leave to cool for 10–15 minutes.

With a serrated knife, cut the logs into slices about 1 cm/³/₈ in thick and lay them on the same baking sheet. Bake in the still-warm oven for a further 10 minutes, until dry and firm.

Leave to cool for 5 minutes or so, before transferring onto a wire rack to cool completely. Store in an airtight container or cookie jar and eat within 1 week.

COFFEE & ALMOND BISCOTTI

The chocolate coffee beans make these lovely little twice-baked biscuits really unusual. There are two kinds of chocolate-covered coffee beans available, one is an actual coffee bean that has been covered in chocolate, the other is simply coffee-flavoured chocolate that has the size, shape and appearance of a coffee bean. Either work well in this recipe, it just depends on how crazy about real coffee you are. I'm an addict, so I love the crunch of the real beans but the latter are lovely, too.

80 g/6 tablespoons butter

80 g/$\frac{1}{2}$ cup blanched almonds

a pinch of salt

350 g/2$\frac{3}{4}$ cups plain/all-purpose flour

150 g/$\frac{3}{4}$ cup caster/granulated sugar

1 small strong espresso

2 eggs, beaten

100 g/$\frac{2}{3}$ cup chocolate coffee beans (chopped, if using chocolate-covered coffee beans as opposed to the type that are just coffee-flavoured chocolate beans)

2–3 baking sheets lined with baking parchment

MAKES 35–40

Preheat the oven to 180°C (350°F) Gas 4.

Put $\frac{1}{2}$ teaspoon of the butter and the almonds into a small frying pan/skillet set over a low heat and cook until the almonds are golden and fragrant. Add the salt, remove from the heat and leave to cool.

In the meantime, put the flour into a large mixing bowl and rub in the remaining butter using fingertips, until it is evenly incorporated. Add the sugar and mix well. Pour in the espresso and stir in the eggs. The mixture should now come together to form a loose dough. Add the chocolate coffee beans.

Divide the dough into three even pieces and shape them into small logs. Pop them onto one of the prepared baking sheets and flatten very slightly.

Bake in the preheated oven for about 20 minutes, until firm and golden. Remove from the oven and leave to cool, but keep the oven on.

With a serrated knife, cut the logs into slices just under 1 cm/$\frac{3}{8}$ in. thick and lay them flat on the remaining baking sheets. Bake in the still-warm oven for a further 10–15 minutes, until dry and crisp.

Remove from the oven, transfer to a wire rack to cool, store in an airtight container or cookie jar and eat within 1 week.

RICCIARELLI

Ricciarelli are heavenly, soft almond cookies that originate in Tuscany, Italy. I first tasted them on a trip to Siena and it was love at first bite. I've seen these lovely cookies in supermarkets outside Italy many times since, but they are so easy to make at home and wonderful eaten fresh from the oven.

250 g/8 oz. marzipan

100 g/$\frac{1}{2}$ cup caster/granulated sugar

1 teaspoon Grand Marnier or other orange liqueur

1 egg white

150 g/1 cup blanched almonds, finely ground

icing/confectioners' sugar, for dusting

a baking sheet lined with baking parchment

MAKES 16–18

Preheat the oven to 180°C (350°F) Gas 4.

Cut the marzipan into small pieces and put in a food processor. Blend to a paste. Add the caster/granulated sugar and Grand Marnier and blend again. Transfer to a large mixing bowl and beat in the egg white. Stir in the ground almonds.

Form the mixture into small logs about 1.5 cm/$\frac{5}{8}$ in. in diameter and 4 cm/ $1\frac{3}{4}$ in. long. Lay them on the prepared baking sheet, leaving room in between each to allow for spreading. Leave to stand in a cool place for about 30 minutes.

Bake in the preheated oven for 8–10 minutes, until golden and firm.

Leave on the baking sheet to cool slightly, and then transfer to a wire rack to cool completely. Dust with icing/confectioners' sugar and serve. Store in an airtight container or cookie jar and eat within 3 days.

pages 68–69
left: ricciarelli
right: amaretti

AMARETTI

Sweet, soft, chewy amaretti biscuits are a real delight with a cup of good coffee – especially a morning espresso! Ground almonds can vary slightly in texture, and so sometimes the mixture may seem a little too wet or too dry. Just remember that the mixture shouldn't be sloppy – nor should it be too solid. Slightly soft and slightly sticky is probably the best way to describe the texture, so if it seems too wet, add more ground almonds and a touch of sugar – or for a mixture that is too dry, a little extra egg white should do the trick.

200 g/1^1/$_3$ cups ground almonds

160 g/^{3}/$_4$ cup caster/granulated sugar

2 egg whites

2–3 drops pure almond extract

50 g/^{1}/$_4$ cup caster/superfine sugar

a baking sheet lined with baking parchment

MAKES ABOUT 20

Preheat the oven to 180°C (350°F) Gas 4.

Mix the ground almonds and caster/granulated sugar together in a large mixing bowl. Stir in the egg whites and almond extract and bring the mixture together to form a soft dough.

Put the caster/superfine sugar into a bowl.

Form the dough into balls the size of small walnuts and roll them gently in the caster/superfine sugar. Arrange on the prepared baking sheets, leaving a little space for spreading between each one.

Bake in the preheated oven for about 15 minutes, until risen, firm and golden.

Leave to cool for a little while on the baking sheet, then transfer to a wire rack and leave to cool completely. Store in an airtight container or cookie jar and eat within 3 days.

LINZER COOKIES

Crisp, buttery cookies sandwiched together with jam/jelly. What bliss. Use your favourite shaped cookie cutter – or a mixture of cutters. I sometimes sandwich these together with lemon curd for a really lovely variation.

130 g/1 stick plus 1 tablespoon butter, softened

130 g/^{2}/$_3$ cup caster/granulated sugar

1 egg

200 g/1^2/$_3$ cups plain/all-purpose flour

100 g/^{2}/$_3$ cup ground almonds

icing/confectioners' sugar, for dusting

100 g/^{1}/$_2$ cup raspberry jam/jelly

2 baking sheets lined with baking parchment

MAKES ABOUT 15

Beat the butter and sugar together in a large mixing bowl until smooth. Add the egg, and continue to beat until fully incorporated. Stir in the flour and almonds and bring the mixture together to form a stiff dough. Cover with clingfilm/plastic wrap and leave to rest for 30 minutes.

Preheat the oven to 180°C (350°F) Gas 4.

On a clean, lightly floured work surface, roll the dough out into a large rectangle about 3–4 mm/^{1}/$_8$ in. thick. Cut out shapes using a cookie cutter. Lay them on the prepared baking sheets, leaving a little space for spreading between each one. At this stage, use a very small cutter to cut out the centre of half the biscuits. Bring the trimmed dough together and roll out again to cut as many cookies out of the dough as possible, making sure you have even numbers of whole cookies and cookies with holes in.

Bake in the preheated oven for about 10 minutes, until light golden and firm.

Leave on the baking sheet to cool slightly, and then transfer to a wire rack to cool completely.

Dust the cookies with holes in with icing/confectioners' sugar. Spread the whole cookies with raspberry jam/jelly and top with the dusted cookies with holes in. Store in an airtight container or cookie jar and eat within 3 days.

VIENNESE WHIRLS

These oh-so-buttery, melt-in-the-mouth biscuits are lovely sandwiched together with buttercream and jam/jelly, but for a simpler version, pipe out the whirls and bake them, then drop a small teaspoon of raspberry jam/jelly into the centre of each without sandwiching the biscuits together.

250 g/2 sticks butter, softened

200 g/1³/₄ cups plain/all-purpose flour (I use Italian 00)

100g/²/₃ cup cornflour/cornstarch

100g/1 cup icing/confectioners' sugar

1 teaspoons pure vanilla extract

icing/confectioners' sugar, to dust

Filling

100 g/1 cup vanilla icing/confectioners' sugar (see Note)

50 g/3¹/₂ tablespoons butter, softened

50 g/¹/₄ cup raspberry jam/jelly

2 baking sheets lined with baking parchment

a piping/pastry bag fitted with a star nozzle/tip

MAKES ABOUT 15

Preheat the oven to 180°C (350°F) Gas 4.

Mix the butter, flours, icing/confectioners' sugar and vanilla together until the mixture forms a smooth dough.

Spoon the mixture into the piping/pastry bag and pipe 30 small ovals, about the size of a small egg, onto the prepared baking sheets, leaving a little space for spreading between each one. I like to do this in a figure of eight for a really pretty pattern.

Bake in the preheated oven for about 15 minutes, until golden.

Remove from the oven and leave to cool for a few minutes, and then transfer to a cooling rack until completely cold.

In the meantime, to make the buttercream filling, simply beat the vanilla icing/confectioners' sugar and butter together in a large mixing bowl until smooth.

Sandwich the biscuits together with a little jam/jelly and buttercream and dust lightly with icing/confectioners' sugar before serving. Store in an airtight container or cookie jar and eat within 3 days.

Note

You can buy ready-made vanilla-flavoured icing/confectioners' sugar or to make your own, simply cut a vanilla pod/bean in half lengthways and add to an airtight container filled with icing/confectioners' sugar. Leave for at least 24 hours before using.

ANZAC BISCUITS

These lovely biscuits first came about when the relatives of the Australian and New Zealand Army Corps serving in Gallipoli wanted something they could send as a gift from home that would keep well. Some recipes for Anzac biscuits call for coconut, but I prefer them without.

100 g/6$^{1}/_{2}$ tablespoons butter

generous 1 tablespoon golden syrup/light corn syrup

125 g/$^{2}/_{3}$ cup caster/granulated sugar

a pinch of salt

100 g/$^{3}/_{4}$ cup self-raising/ self-rising flour

1 teaspoon bicarbonate of soda/ baking soda

180 g/1$^{1}/_{4}$ cups jumbo rolled oats

2 baking sheets lined with baking parchment

MAKES 15

Preheat the oven to 180°C (350°F) Gas 4.

Melt the butter, golden syrup/light corn syrup, sugar and salt together in a saucepan set over a low heat.

Put the flour, bicarbonate of soda/baking soda and oats into a mixing bowl. Pour in the melted butter mixture and stir in 2 tablespoons water.

Form the cookie mixture into balls the size of walnuts and place on the prepared baking sheets, leaving a little space for spreading between each one. Press down gently to flatten them slightly.

Bake in the preheated oven for 12–15 minutes, until the cookies are firm.

Transfer to a wire rack to cool, store in an airtight container or cookie jar and eat within 1 week.

VANILLA KIPFERLS

These deliciously short, crumbly little crescent-shaped cookies originated in Austria, but are popular throughout northern Europe around Christmas time. A liberal dusting of icing/confectioners' sugar gives them their distinctive look and adds to their lovely delicate flavour.

140 g/1 stick plus
   1¹/₂ tablespoons butter,
   softened
60 g/¹/₄ cup plus 1 tablespoon
   caster/granulated sugar
1 teaspoon pure vanilla extract
160 g/1¹/₄ cups plain/all-purpose
   flour
100 g/²/₃ cup ground almonds
icing/confectioners' sugar,
   for dusting

*a baking sheet lined with baking
   parchment*

MAKES ABOUT 20

Preheat the oven to 180°C (350°F) Gas 4.

Beat the butter and sugar together in a large mixing bowl until smooth. Stir in the vanilla extract. Add the flour and ground almonds, and mix everything together until you have a soft, smooth dough.

Form the dough into balls the size of walnuts and roll each into a small sausage shape. Bend the sausage to create a crescent shape and arrange carefully on the baking sheet, leaving a little space for spreading between each one.

Bake in the preheated oven for about 10 minutes, until golden and firm.

Leave to cool slightly on the baking sheet and then transfer to a wire rack until completely cold. Dust with icing/confectioners' sugar to serve. Store in an airtight container or cookie jar and eat within 5 days.

ALMENDRADOS

You could almost say that these soft, chewy, traditional Spanish almond cookies are cousins to Italian amaretti, but a liberal speckling of lemon zest and the whole egg used to bind them gives them a deliciously different finish.

200 g/1¹/₃ cups ground almonds

175 g/³/₄ cup plus 2 tablespoons caster/granulated sugar

grated zest of 1 lemon, finely grated

1 egg, beaten

12 whole blanched almonds

a baking sheet lined with baking parchment

MAKES 12

Preheat the oven to 180°C (350°F) Gas 4.

Put the ground almonds into a large mixing bowl and add 150 g/³/₄ cup of the sugar and the lemon zest. Add the egg, and bring the mixture together to form a smooth, slightly sticky dough.

Put the remaining sugar in a wide, shallow dish and set aside.

Form the mixture into 12 balls the size of walnuts and roll each ball in the remaining sugar.

Place the balls onto the prepared baking sheet, leaving a little space for spreading between each one. Push a whole almond into the centre of each ball and bake in the preheated oven for 8–10 minutes, until the cookies feel firm on the outside, but are still soft in the centre and have a very pale golden colour.

Remove from the oven and leave to cool for 5 minutes or so, before transferring to a wire rack to cool completely. Store in an airtight container or cookie jar and eat within 5 days.

BRETON BISCUITS

Light and buttery, these wonderful biscuits are based on the very popular traditional French biscuits known as 'galettes Bretonnes'. They're lovely with a cuppa, but great to serve alongside creamy desserts and ice creams, too.

130 g/1 stick plus 1 tablespoon butter, softened

130 g/^{2}/$_3$ cup caster/granulated sugar

seeds from 1 vanilla pod/bean

230 g/1^3/$_4$ cups plain/all-purpose flour

1 teaspoon baking powder

1 egg, beaten

1 egg white, beaten

30 g/2^1/$_2$ tablespoons caster/superfine sugar

Chocolate variation

130 g/1 stick plus 1 tablespoon butter, softened

130 g/^{2}/$_3$ cup caster/granulated sugar

25 g/3 tablespoons unsweetened cocoa powder

200 g/1^3/$_4$ cups plain/all-purpose flour

1 teaspoon baking powder

1 egg, beaten

1 egg white, beaten

2 baking sheets lined with baking parchment

MAKES ABOUT 25

Preheat the oven to 180°C (350°F) Gas 4.

Beat the butter, sugar and vanilla seeds together in a large mixing bowl until smooth. Add the flour and baking powder, and then the egg. Mix until everything is fully combined and then bring together to form a soft dough.

Lay two pieces of clingfilm/plastic wrap on a clean work surface and lightly dust with flour. Divide the mixture in two and roll into long sausage shapes, about 4 cm/1^3/$_4$ in. in diameter. Wrap them tightly in the clingfilm/plastic wrap and twist the edges to seal. Refrigerate for 30 minutes or so, until the dough has firmed up a little.

Meanwhile, mix together the beaten egg white and caster/superfine sugar in a small mixing bowl to make an egg glaze.

Unwrap the dough and cut into 1 cm/^{3}/$_8$ in. slices. Brush the egg glaze over each biscuit and lay the slices on the prepared baking sheet.

Bake in the preheated oven for 8–10 minutes, until golden and firm.

Cool on a wire rack, store in an airtight container or cookie jar and eat within 1 week.

Variation
To make chocolate Bretons, preheat the oven to 180°C (350°F) Gas 4.

Beat the butter and caster/granulated sugar together in a large mixing bowl until smooth. Add the cocoa, flour and baking powder, and then the whole egg. Mix until everything is fully combined and then bring together to form a soft dough.

Follow the instructions as above for rolling, cutting, glazing and baking these delicious little biscuits.

LOVER'S KNOTS

Lover's knots are traditionally eaten in Italy to celebrate Carnivale, a festival held just before Lent. They make a nice change from the other baked cookies that feature in this book and will make a lovely addition to any cookie fan's repertoire. Delicious served freshly cooked with a cup of good coffee, they are also perfect to serve alongside creamy desserts.

250 g/2 cups plain/all-purpose flour

40 g/3 tablespoons caster/granulated sugar

finely grated zest of 1 orange

2 tablespoons Grand Marnier (or other orange liqueur)

40 g/2^1/$_2$ tablespoons butter, melted

1 whole egg, beaten

1 egg yolk

sunflower oil, for deep frying

caster/superfine sugar, for dusting

a baking sheet lined with baking parchment

MAKES ABOUT 25

Put the flour, sugar and orange zest into a large mixing bowl. Add the Grand Marnier, melted butter, beaten egg and egg yolk, and mix everything together to form a soft dough. Cover with clingfilm/plastic wrap and leave the dough to rest for 1 hour.

On a clean, lightly floured work surface, roll the dough out into a large rectangle about 5 mm/^{3}/$_{16}$ in. thick. Cut into ribbons about 1 cm/^{3}/$_8$ in. wide and 8 cm/3^1/$_4$ in. long. Carefully tie a knot into the centre of each ribbon and transfer to the prepared baking sheet, leaving a little room around each.

Heat some oil in a heavy-bottomed saucepan or wok over a medium heat to a temperature of 190°C (375°F). Fry the knots in batches, until crisp and golden.

Remove the knots from the oil using a slotted spoon and drain on paper towels. Dust with caster/superfine sugar to serve or store in an airtight container or cookie jar and eat within 5 days.

SCOTTISH SHORTBREAD

Traditional Scottish shortbread is made using a 3:2:1 ratio. I've sneaked in a little extra butter and some vanilla to make this very crumbly, buttery, hellishly addictive version. All the recipes in this book are made with salted butter, and it really is important here as it heightens the flavour beautifully.

300 g/2¹/₃ cups plain/all-purpose flour

240 g/2 sticks butter, softened

100 g/1 cup icing/confectioners' sugar

seeds from 2 vanilla pods or ¹/₂ teaspoon vanilla bean paste

caster/superfine sugar, for dusting

a small baking sheet lined with baking parchment

MAKES 12

Preheat the oven to 180°C (350°F) Gas 4.

Put all the ingredients in a large mixing bowl and work everything together to form a smooth dough.

On a clean, lightly floured work surface, roll the dough out into a large 16 cm/6¹/₂ in. square about 1 cm/³/₈ in. thick. Cut the dough into 12 fingers and, with a narrow metal spatula, transfer them to the prepared baking sheet, leaving a little room around each. Refrigerate for 30 minutes.

Bake in the preheated oven for 10–15 minutes, until firm and pale golden.

Remove from the oven and prick holes into the top of the shortbread using the tines of a fork. Dust with caster/superfine sugar and leave to cool for 5 minutes. Transfer to a wire rack and leave to cool completely. Store in an airtight container or cookie jar and eat within 5 days.

OAT & SPELT BISCUITS

These are my version of the much loved biscuits we Brits know as a 'digestives', a kind of cousin to America's famous graham cracker. They're most often made from wholemeal flour and oatmeal, but I have used spelt flour and whole oat flakes, which I think gives them a lovely light texture and delicious flavour. They're great eaten unadorned with a cuppa but make a perfect accompaniment to cheese – and if you're feeling a little indulgent, a coating of milk/semi-sweet or dark/bittersweet chocolate makes them very special indeed.

175 g/1 $^1/_3$ cups spelt flour

150 g/1 generous cup whole oat flakes

50 g/$^1/_4$ cup Demerara/turbinado sugar

a pinch of salt

$^1/_2$ teaspoon bicarbonate of soda/ baking soda

150 g/1 stick plus 2 tablespoons butter, softened

a 4–5 cm/1 $^3/_4$–2 in. round cookie cutter

2 baking sheets lined with baking parchment

MAKES ABOUT 25

Preheat the oven to 180°C (350°F) Gas 4.

Mix the flour, oat flakes and sugar together in a large mixing bowl. Add the salt and bicarbonate of soda/baking soda. Rub in the butter until it is evenly incorporated and draw the mixture together to form a smooth but not sticky dough. Wrap the dough in clingfilm/plastic wrap and pop in the fridge for 30 minutes or so to firm up a little.

On a clean, lightly floured work surface, roll the dough out into a large rectangle with a thickness of about 3 mm/$^1/_8$ in. Cut out circles using the cookie cutter. Bring the trimmed dough together and roll out again to cut as many cookies out of the dough as possible.

Arrange the cookies on the prepared baking sheets and bake in the preheated oven for 10–15 minutes, until firm and golden.

Leave to cool for about 5 minutes or so, before transferring to a wire rack to cool completely. Store in an airtight container or cookie jar and eat within 5 days.

ROSEMARY & PECORINO COOKIES

These Italian-inspired savoury cookies are fabulous to serve alongside pre-dinner drinks and are also nice as part of an Italian cheese board.

180 g/1$\frac{1}{3}$ cups plain/all-purpose flour

a pinch of salt

1 tablespoon finely chopped rosemary

180 g/1$\frac{3}{4}$ cups finely grated Pecorino romano cheese

180 g/1$\frac{1}{2}$ sticks butter, softened

2 baking sheets lined with baking parchment

MAKES ABOUT 25

Preheat the oven to 180°C (350°F) Gas 4.

Put the flour, salt and rosemary into a large mixing bowl. Add the butter and work it into the flour. Add the cheese and draw everything together to form a smooth, soft dough.

Lay two pieces of clingfilm/plastic wrap on a clean work surface. Lightly dust with flour. Divide the mixture into two pieces and roll into long sausage shapes, about 2.5 cm/1 in. in diameter. Wrap them tightly in the clingfilm/plastic wrap and twist the edges to seal. Refrigerate for 15 minutes or so, until the dough has firmed up a little.

Unwrap the dough and cut into 3 mm/$\frac{1}{8}$ in. slices. Lay the slices the prepared baking sheet and bake in the preheated oven for 6–8 minutes, until golden and firm.

Cool on a wire rack, store in an airtight container or cookie jar and eat within 3 days.

GARIBALDIS

We used to have these at home all the time when I was growing up. They remind me a little bit of Eccles cakes – the round crumbly pastries filled with currants that my Dad always used to call 'fly pies'. I like to try to get as many currants into the centre of the dough as possible.

225 g/1³/₄ cups plain/all-purpose flour

¹/₂ teaspoon baking powder

60 g/¹/₂ stick butter, softened

60 g/5 tablespoons Demerara/turbinado sugar

4–5 tablespoons milk

150 g/1 cup Zante currants

1 egg white, beaten

caster/superfine sugar, for dusting

2 baking sheets lined with baking parchment

MAKES 16

Preheat the oven to 180°C (350°F) Gas 4.

Put the flour into a large mixing bowl and stir in the baking powder. Rub the butter into the flour until it resembles fine breadcrumbs. Stir in the sugar, add the milk and bring everything together to form a soft dough.

On a clean, lightly floured work surface, roll the dough out into a large rectangle with a thickness of about 3 mm/¹/₈ in. Cut it into two pieces both measuring the same size. Scatter the currants over one half of the dough. Brush the remaining dough lightly with water and place it carefully, brushed-side down over the currants. Gently roll the rolling pin across the top of the dough until you can see the currants through the top and both layers seem firmly stuck together.

Brush the surface with the beaten egg white and scatter with caster/superfine sugar. Cut the dough into 16 rectangles and mark each garibaldi with a few little holes using the tines of a fork.

Arrange on the prepared baking sheets and bake in the preheated oven for 10–15 minutes, until golden and firm.

Cool for 5–10 minutes on the baking sheets and then transfer to a wire rack to cool completely. Store in an airtight container or cookie jar and eat within 3 days.

SNICKERDOODLES

Snickerdoodles quite possibly originated in Germany, but now these crunchy, cinnamon sugar-coated cookies are most popular in the USA. Cream of tartar is an essential ingredient in the authentic Snickerdoodle, but it should be easy enough to find in good supermarkets.

220 g/1³/₄ cups plain/ all-purpose flour

120 g/1 stick butter

90 g/scant ¹/₂ cup soft brown sugar

2 teaspoons baking powder

1 teaspoon cream of tartar

2 eggs, beaten

2 tablespoons white sugar

2 teaspoons ground cinnamon

2 baking sheets lined with baking parchment

MAKES ABOUT 20

Preheat the oven to 180°C (350°F) Gas 4.

Rub the flour and butter together in a large mixing bowl until the mixture resembles fine breadcrumbs. Stir in the sugar, baking powder and cream of tartar. Add the eggs and draw the mixture together to form a soft dough.

Form the mixture into balls the size of walnuts.

Mix the sugar and ground cinnamon together in a wide, shallow dish. Roll the balls in the cinnamon sugar and arrange on the prepared baking sheets, leaving a little space for spreading between each one.

Bake in the preheated oven for about 15 minutes, until golden and firm.

Leave to cool for 5 minutes, and then transfer to a wire rack until completely cold. Store in an airtight container or cookie jar and eat within 5 days.

CHOCOLATE PRETZELS

I sometimes ring the changes by cutting the quantity of ground almonds down to 60 g/ $^1/_2$ cup and adding 40 g/$^1/_3$ cup cocoa powder. It may take a little practice to get the pretzel shape but once you get the hang of it, these lovely cookies are a doddle to make!

125 g/1 stick butter

250 g/2 cups plain/all-purpose flour

100 g/$^2/_3$ cup ground almonds

85 g/scant $^1/_2$ cup caster/ granulated sugar

2 eggs

150 g/5 oz. good-quality dark/bittersweet chocolate, for coating

2 baking sheets lined with baking parchment

MAKES ABOUT 25

Preheat the oven to 180°C (350°F) Gas 4.

Rub the butter and flour together in a large mixing bowl until the mixture resembles fine breadcrumbs. Add the ground almonds and sugar. Stir in the eggs and mix until the dough comes together to create a soft dough.

Divide the dough into small balls and roll each out into very thin sausages. Form each sausage into a pretzel shape by bringing the ends upwards and toward the centre (as if you were forming a circle), cross over the ends, twist and connect each end to the opposite side of the loop. Lift them gently onto the prepared baking sheets, leaving a little room between each.

Bake in the preheated oven for about 10 minutes, until firm and golden.

Cool on a wire rack.

Melt the chocolate in a bowl set over a pan of barely simmering water, then dip the pretzels into the melted chocolate to coat. Leave to set on a wire rack. Store in an airtight container in a cool place (but not the fridge), so the chocolate doesn't melt, and eat within 3 days.

IT'S HOLIDAY SEASON

LEMON & VANILLA YOGURT HEARTS WITH FONDANT ICING

Fondant icing/confectioners' sugar is available from large supermarkets and specialist cake decorating shops, but you could also use the ready-to-roll fondant icing and simply knead in a drop or two of food colouring before rolling out.

200 g/1²/₃ cups plain/all-purpose flour

a pinch of salt

90 g/6 tablespoons butter

seeds from 1 vanilla pod/bean

1 teaspoon finely grated lemon zest

50 ml/3¹/₂ tablespoons thick plain yogurt

Fondant icing

175 g/1³/₄ cups fondant icing/ confectioners' sugar

red food colouring

2 baking sheets lined with baking parchment

heart-shaped cookie cutters in various sizes

1–2 disposable piping/pastry bags

MAKES ABOUT 20

Preheat the oven to 180°C (350°F) Gas 4.

Put the flour and salt into a large mixing bowl and add the vanilla seeds and lemon zest. Mix well. Rub in the butter until it is thoroughly incorporated. Stir in the yogurt and bring the mixture together to form a soft dough.

On a clean, lightly floured work surface, roll the dough out into a large rectangle about 4 mm/¹/₈ in. thick. Cut out hearts with the cutters and arrange on the prepared baking sheets, leaving a little space for spreading between each one. Bring the trimmed dough together and roll out again to cut as many hearts out of the dough as possible. Arrange on the baking sheets with the other cookies.

Bake in the preheated oven for about 10 minutes, until golden and firm.

Remove from the oven and transfer to a wire rack to cool.

Mix 100 g/1 cup of the fondant icing/confectioners' sugar with enough water and food colouring to create a fairly thick paste, making sure it is a pretty delicate pink and not too Barbie pink and decorate the biscuits by creating a heart shape a little smaller than the shape of the biscuit, leaving a small border (you could use a piping/pastry bag for this or simply spread with a palette knife). Mix the remaining fondant icing/confectioners' sugar with enough water to make a thick paste and pipe little white dots to create a pretty outline around the pink sugar icing.

Leave to set, store between layers of baking parchment in an airtight container or cookie jar and eat within 3 days.

SPICED PUMPKIN COOKIES

100 g/6¹/₂ tablespoons butter,
softened

60 g/¹/₄ cup thick honey

150 g/³/₄ cup soft brown sugar

1 egg

250 g/2 cups plain/all-purpose
flour

1 teaspoon mixed spice/apple pie
spice

1 teaspoon ground ginger

¹/₂ teaspoon bicarbonate of
soda/baking soda

To decorate

250 g/8 oz. ready-to-roll fondant
icing

orange food colouring gel

1 egg white, beaten

orange and green writing gels

a pumpkin-shaped cookie cutter

*2 baking sheets lined with
baking parchment*

MAKES ABOUT 20

These are lovely, lightly spiced cookies that look great cut into pumpkin shapes – perfect for Halloween or Thanksgiving.

Preheat the oven to 180°C (350°F) Gas 4.

Put the butter, honey, sugar and egg in a large mixing bowl and beat together until smooth. Add the flour, spices and bicarbonate of soda/baking soda and mix until you have a smooth, stiff dough. Leave the dough to rest for 30 minutes.

On a clean, lightly floured work surface, roll the dough out into a large rectangle with a thickness of about 3 mm/¹/₈ in. Cut out cookies using the cookie cutter. Bring the trimmed dough together and roll out again to cut as many cookies out of the dough as possible. Arrange the cookies on the prepared baking sheets, leaving a little space for spreading between each one.

Bake in the preheated oven for 8–10 minutes, until golden and firm. Leave to cool slightly before transferring to a wire rack to cool completely.

In the meantime, work a little orange food colouring gel into the fondant icing until the colour resembles pumpkin orange. Cut the icing out using the cookie cutter to cover the cookies.

Brush the cookies with the beaten egg white and stick an orange icing pumpkin onto each cookie pumpkin, then use the writing gels to add the detail.

Leave to set, store between layers of baking parchment in an airtight container or cookie jar and eat within 3 days.

LEMON & CHOCOLATE EASTER BUNNIES

For these sweet little children's Easter cookies, I use a 3-D mould that makes them look especially pretty (see Suppliers on page 11 and 192). They are perfect to make with children during Lent, in the run-up to Easter, and make a really cute gift tied up with ribbon in cellophane bags. Everyone loves chocolate at Easter time, and the chocolate variation are delicious. I like to make both and serve them together.

250 g/2 sticks butter

125 g/²/₃ cup caster/granulated sugar

finely grated zest of 2 lemons

250 g/2 cups plain/all-purpose flour

125 g/1 cup rice flour

caster/superfine sugar, for dusting

Chocolate variation

250 g/2 sticks butter

125 g/²/₃ cup caster/granulated sugar

225 g/1³/₄ cups plain/all-purpose flour

125 g/1 cup rice flour

25 g/3 tablespoons unsweetened cocoa powder

caster/superfine sugar, for dusting

2 baking sheets lined with baking parchment

1–2 bunny-shaped cookie cutters

MAKES ABOUT 50

Preheat the oven to 180°C (350°F) Gas 4.

Beat the butter, sugar and lemon zest together in a large mixing bowl, and then work in the flours until the mixture comes together to form a soft, smooth dough.

On a clean, lightly floured work surface, roll the dough out into a large rectangle about 3–4 mm/¹/₈ in. thick. Cut out bunnies using the cookie cutter. Bring the trimmed dough together and roll out again to cut as many cookies out of the dough as possible. Lay them on the prepared baking sheets, leaving a little space for spreading between each one.

Bake in the preheated oven for about 8 minutes, until firm and golden (the baking time will depend on the size of the cutter used).

Remove the cookies from the oven and leave to cool for several minutes on the baking sheet, before transferring to a wire rack to cool completely. Dust with caster/superfine sugar to serve or store in an airtight container or cookie jar and eat within 5 days.

VARIATION

To make chocolate bunnies, preheat the oven to 180°C (350°F) Gas 4.

Beat the butter and sugar together in a large mixing bowl, and then work in the flours and the cocoa powder, until the mixture comes together to form a soft, smooth dough.

Follow the instructions as above for rolling, cutting and baking the bunnies.

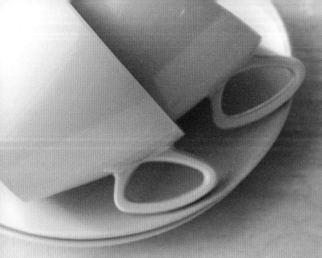

FRUITED EASTER BISCUITS

I remember these lovely, crisp sugar-coated cookies were known as 'Shrewsbury biscuits' when I was growing up. Buttery and lemony, with a delightful speckling of chewy currants, I still have a soft spot for them now. They're great to eat throughout the year, but if you're making them at Easter with children in mind, then it's lovely to use shaped cookie cutters such as ducks and lambs.

120 g/1 stick butter

120 g/1 cup plus 2 tablespoons caster/granulated sugar

180 g/1¹/₃ cups plain/all-purpose flour

finely grated zest of 1 lemon

50 g/¹/₃ cup Zante currants

1 egg, separated

caster/superfine sugar, for dusting

a cookie cutter

2 baking sheets lined with baking parchment

MAKES ABOUT 18

Preheat the oven to 180°C (350°F) Gas 4.

Put the butter, sugar and flour together in a large mixing bowl. Rub together until the mixture resembles fine breadcrumbs. Add the lemon zest and the currants and stir until evenly mixed, and then add the egg yolk. Bring everything together to form a smooth dough.

On a clean, lightly floured work surface, roll the dough out into a large rectangle with a thickness of about 3 mm/¹/₈ in. Cut out cookies using the cutters of your choice. Bring the trimmed dough together and roll out again to cut as many cookies out of the dough as possible. Arrange the cookies on the prepared baking sheets, leaving a little space for spreading between each one.

Beat the egg white a little and brush the biscuits lightly with it. Sprinkle with caster/superfine sugar and bake in the preheated oven for 8–10 minutes, until golden and firm.

Remove from the oven and leave to cool on the baking sheets for 10 minutes or so, before transferring to a wire rack to cool completely. Store in an airtight container or cookie jar and eat within 5 days.

BUTTER COOKIE BATS

These buttery cookies look fabulous around Halloween time – bat cookie cutters can be found at good kitchen supply shops and children will love them!

**300 g/2¹/₃ cups plain/
  all-purpose flour**
240 g/2 sticks butter, softened
**100 g/1 cup icing/confectioners'
  sugar**

To decorate

black ready-to-roll fondant icing
1 egg white, lightly beaten
black and white writing gels

a bat-shaped cookie cutter

*a baking sheet lined with baking
  parchment*

MAKES ABOUT 12

Preheat the oven to 180°C (350°F) Gas 4.

Put all the ingredients in a large mixing bowl and work everything together to form a smooth dough.

On a clean, lightly floured work surface, roll the dough out into a large 10 cm/ 4 in. square with a thickness of about 7 mm/¹/₄ in. Cut out cookies using the cookie cutter. Bring the trimmed dough together and roll out again to cut as many cookies out of the dough as possible. Arrange the cookies on the prepared baking sheets, leaving a little space for spreading between each one.

Bake in the preheated oven for 8–10 minutes, until firm and pale golden. Remove from the oven and leave to cool on the baking sheets for 5 minutes or so, before transferring to a wire rack to cool completely.

Roll out the fondant icing and cut into bat shapes using the cookie cutter. Brush the biscuits lightly with the egg white and stick a black icing bat onto each cookie bat. Decorate each one by adding eyes with the black and white writing gels.

Leave to set, store between layers of baking parchment in an airtight container or cookie jar and eat within 3 days.

WITCHES' FINGERS

These crumbly, buttery biscuits with a hint of cinnamon are delicious – and they're brilliant fun for children to make at Halloween as the whole almonds look very realistic as witches' fingernails! Make the biscuits quite knobbly and uneven to be even more accurate!

190 g/1 1/2 cups plain/all-purpose flour

135 g/1 stick plus 1 tablespoon butter, softened, plus a little extra to bring the mixture together if necessary

100 g/1 scant cup icing/confectioners' sugar

1/2 teaspoon ground cinnamon

1/2 teaspoon baking powder

whole blanched almonds, for the fingernails

Cinnamon sugar

2 tablespoons caster/superfine sugar

1/4 teaspoon ground cinnamon

a baking sheet lined with baking parchment

MAKES ABOUT 15

Preheat the oven to 180°C (350°F) Gas 4.

Put all the ingredients in a large mixing bowl and work everything together to form a smooth dough. If still a little dry, add an extra 1/2 tablespoon softened butter at a time until you can work with the dough.

Form long, bobbly finger shapes and arrange on the prepared baking sheet. Place a whole almond at the top of each finger to look like a fingernail and scores lines at two points to look like finger joints.

Bake in the preheated oven for 8–10 minutes, until firm and pale golden.

Remove from the oven and leave to cool on the baking sheets for 5 minutes or so, before transferring to a wire rack to cool completely.

Mix the caster/superfine sugar and cinnamon together and scatter over the fingers to serve. Store in an airtight container or cookie jar and eat within 5 days.

PEANUT CRUNCH

If you're a peanut addict like me, you'll agree that there's simply no point having a peanut cookie that isn't chock-full of peanuts. This one fits the bill nicely. In fact, I did try to cram a few more in, but when it got to the point where they were falling back into the bowl and I was eating them, I realized it might be a better idea to use very slightly less and just eat the leftover nuts out of the packet. Well, cook's perks and all that...

85 g/6 tablespoons butter

150/^{3}/$_4$ cup Demerara/turbinado sugar

1 egg, beaten

150 g/1 cup plus 2^1/$_2$ tablespoons plain/all-purpose flour

a pinch of salt

150 g/1 cup salted peanuts

2 baking sheets lined with baking parchment

MAKES ABOUT 20

Preheat the oven to 180°C (350°F) Gas 4.

Beat the butter and sugar together in a large mixing bowl until smooth. Add the egg. Stir in the flour and salt and work everything together to form a smooth dough. Add the peanuts and work gently but thoroughly into the dough until evenly incorporated.

Form the mixture into balls the size of walnuts and arrange them on the prepared baking sheets, leaving a little space for spreading between each one. Flatten the cookies slightly with the tines of a fork.

Bake in the preheated oven for about 10 minutes, until golden and firm.

Leave to cool on the baking sheets for 5 minutes, before transferring to a wire rack to cool completely. Store in an airtight container or cookie jar and eat within 5 days.

SPICE COOKIES

140 g/1 stick plus
   1 1/2 tablespoons butter,
   softened

100 g/1/2 cup caster/granulated
   sugar

80 g/scant 1/2 cup dark
   muscovado sugar (or molasses
   sugar)

1 egg yolk, beaten

150 g/1 cup plus
   2 1/2 tablespoons plain/
   all-purpose flour

1 teaspoon bicarbonate of soda/
   baking soda

1 teaspoon ground ginger

1/2 teaspoon ground cinnamon

scant 1/2 teaspoon mixed spice/
   apple pie spice

a pinch of salt

caster/superfine sugar, for
   sprinkling

*2 baking sheets lined with
   baking parchment*

MAKES ABOUT 20

I love spice cookies. Something quite magical happens when you combine dark, sticky, toffee-ish muscovado sugar with mixed sweet spices. I have them ('them' usually means two as I can't seem to stop at one) with a cup of tea, but often try to eat them standing up, because anything eaten standing up doesn't really count, does it?

Preheat the oven to 180°C (350°F) Gas 4.

Cream the butter and sugars together in a large mixing bowl until smooth. Add the egg yolk and stir until well mixed.

In a separate bowl, mix the flour, bicarbonate of soda/baking soda, spices and salt together. Add to the wet ingredients and mix thoroughly.

Form the mixture into a log with a diameter of about 8–9 cm/3 1/2 in., then refrigerate for 30 minutes or so, to firm up.

Cut the dough into slices about 7 mm/1/4 in. thick and lay on the prepared baking sheets, leaving a little space for spreading between each one.

Bake in the preheated oven for 12–14 minutes, until firm.

Leave to cool on the baking sheets – the cookies will crisp up as they cool. Sprinkle with caster/superfine sugar to serve or store in an airtight container or cookie jar and eat within 5 days.

LEMON SNOWFLAKES

These lovely lemony cookies are perfect at Christmas time, and the snowflake shape gives them such a pretty, elegant look. I like to decorate them in a mixture of ways – some I cover completely with icing/frosting, and others, I trace the skeleton of the shape using a writing tube and piping/pastry bag. However you choose to decorate them, they're sure to be a hit. And if you want to make them at times other than in winter, then just use a different cookie cutter!

250 g/2 cups plain/all-purpose flour

125 g/1 cup cornflour/cornstarch

125 g/^{2}/3 cup caster/granulated sugar

grated zest of 1 large lemon

250 g/2 sticks butter, softened

Royal icing

1 egg white

freshly squeezed juice of 1 lemon

200 g/2 cups icing/confectioners' sugar

snowflake-shaped cookie cutters in various sizes

2 baking sheets lined with baking parchment

a piping/pastry bag fitted with a writing nozzle/tip

MAKES ABOUT 20

Preheat the oven to 180°C (350°F) Gas 4.

Put the dry ingredients and lemon zest into a large mixing bowl and stir well. Add the butter and using your hands work the mixture into a smooth dough.

On a clean, lightly floured work surface, roll the dough out into a large rectangle about 3–4 mm/^{1}/8 in. thick. Cut out snowflakes using the cookie cutters. Lay them on the prepared baking sheets, leaving a little space for spreading between each one. Bring the trimmed dough together and roll out again to cut as many cookies out of the dough as possible. Arrange on the baking sheets with the other cookies.

Bake in the preheated oven for 8–10 minutes, until golden and firm.

Leave to cool slightly on the baking sheets, and then transfer to a wire rack until completely cold.

Lightly whip the egg white in a large mixing bowl and beat in the lemon juice and icing/confectioners' sugar. Transfer the mixture to the piping/pastry bag and decorate the cookies as desired.

Leave to set, store between layers of baking parchment in an airtight container or cookie jar and eat within 3 days.

pages 114–115
left: lemon snowflakes
right: pistachio Christmas trees

PISTACHIO CHRISTMAS TREES

These crunchy, pretty little pistachio-coated trees look really festive around Christmas time and are great packaged up in pretty cellophane bags and tied with ribbon to give as edible gifts to friends and family.

125 g/1 stick butter

125 g/^{2}/$_3$ cup caster/granulated sugar

1 whole egg

250 g/2 cups plain/all-purpose flour

1 egg white, lightly beaten

100 g/^{3}/$_4$ cup finely chopped pistachios

icing/confectioners' sugar, for dusting (optional)

2 baking sheets lined with baking parchment

Christmas tree-shaped cookie cutters in various sizes

MAKES 20–25

Preheat the oven to 180°C (350°F) Gas 4.

Beat the butter and sugar together in a large mixing bowl until smooth. Add the whole egg and beat until fully incorporated. Stir in the flour and bring the mixture together to make a soft, but not sticky dough. Wrap in clingfilm/plastic wrap and chill in the fridge for 30 minutes.

On a clean, lightly floured work surface, roll the dough out into a large rectangle about 3–4 mm/^{1}/$_8$ in. thick. Cut out Christmas trees using the cookie cutters. Lay them on the prepared baking sheets, leaving a little space for spreading between each one. Bring the trimmed dough together and roll out again to cut as many cookies out of the dough as possible. Arrange on the baking sheets with the other cookies.

Brush the top of each cookie with the lightly beaten egg white, leaving the trunk of the tree without the egg white wash. Scatter the chopped pistachios over the branch part of the tree to decorate.

Bake in the preheated oven for 10–15 minutes, until golden and firm.

Leave to cool on the baking sheets for 5 minutes or so, before transferring to a wire rack to cool completely.

I like to dust these with icing/confectioners' sugar to emulate fresh snow. Store between layers of baking parchment in an airtight container or cookie jar and eat within 3 days.

COCONUT SNOWBALLS

These look so pretty. Coconut fans will love them. Sometimes I coat the finished cookies in white chocolate rather than marmalade, although I think I'm personally biased towards the marmalade version.

100 g/6$\frac{1}{2}$ tablespoons butter, softened

150 g/$\frac{3}{4}$ cup caster/granulated sugar

1 egg

200 g/1$\frac{2}{3}$ cups plain/all-purpose flour

1 generous teaspoon baking powder

finely grated zest of 1 orange

Coconut coating

100 g/scant $\frac{1}{2}$ cup seedless orange marmalade

150 g/1$\frac{1}{3}$ cups desiccated/shredded coconut

2 baking sheets lined with baking parchment

MAKES 25–30

Preheat the oven to 180°C (350°F) Gas 4.

Beat the butter and sugar together in a large mixing bowl until smooth. Add the egg, and continue to beat until fully incorporated. Stir in the flour, baking powder and orange zest and bring the mixture together to form a stiff dough.

Roll the mixture into small balls the size of walnuts and lay on the prepared baking sheets, leaving a little space for spreading between each one. Pat down lightly for a flat finish (as pictured) or leave ball-shaped for a snowball bite.

Bake in the preheated oven for about 10 minutes, until light golden and firm.

Leave on the baking sheet for 5 minutes or so to cool slightly, and then transfer to a wire rack to cool completely.

Put the dessicated/shredded coconut in a wide, shallow dish and set aside.

When the snowballs are cold, gently warm the marmalade in a small saucepan set over a low heat and brush it over the entire surface of the snowballs. Roll in the coconut to coat and leave to set.

Store in an airtight container or cookie jar and eat within 1 week.

CHRISTMAS TREE STACK

A lovely stack of crisp, buttery cookies, made to look like an elegant Christmas tree is a very special thing to make for Christmas. You can buy individual star cookie cutters in descending sizes, or search out the kits that are especially made for the purpose. These usually include about 10 cookie cutters from very large for the base, to very tiny ones for the top.

120 g/1 stick butter

120 g/^{2}/$_3$ cup caster/granulated sugar

180 g/1^1/$_3$ cups plain/all-purpose flour

1 egg yolk

500 g/16 oz. white ready-to-roll fondant icing (or use green coloured if preferred)

50 g/^{1}/$_4$ cup apricot jam/jelly, strained

50 g/^{1}/$_2$ cup icing/confectioners' sugar

star-shaped cookie cutters in various sizes

2 baking sheets lined with baking parchment

MAKES 1

Preheat the oven to 180°C (350°F) Gas 4.

Put the butter, sugar and flour in a large mixing bowl. Rub together until the mixture resembles fine breadcrumbs, and then add the egg yolk. Bring everything together to form a smooth dough.

On a clean, lightly floured work surface, roll out the dough into a large rectangle about 4 mm/^{1}/$_8$ in. thick. Cut out star shapes in descending sizes. Bring the trimmed dough together and roll out again to cut as many cookies out of the dough as possible. Arrange the biscuits on the prepared baking sheets, with the larger cookies on one sheet and the smaller cookies on another.

Bake the larger cookies in the preheated oven for 8–10 minutes, and the smaller for 4–8 minutes, until golden and firm.

Leave to cool on the baking sheets for 10 minutes or so, before transferring to a wire rack until completely cold.

Roll out the fondant icing and cut into stars using the cookie cutters, so that you have fondant stars that correspond in size to the cookies.

Brush the cold cookies with apricot jam/jelly (heat it up a little in a saucepan set over a low heat if the jam/jelly is too thick to brush) and place the matching fondant star on top. Push gently to secure, taking care not to break the cookies.

Stack the cookies on top of each other, starting with the largest cookie at the base. Mix the icing/confectioners' sugar with enough water to create a thick icing and decorate the finished tree with sweets and silver balls, using the icing to secure them.

STAINED GLASS WINDOW BISCUITS

These cookies are so pretty, easy to make and are great fun to bake with children for a special treat at Christmas time. Make holes in the top before baking so that you can push pretty ribbon through and hang them from the Christmas tree. Buy the packs of multi-coloured boiled sweets/hard candies, and keep the colours separate for the best effect.

175 g/1⅓ cups plain/all-purpose flour

50 g/3½ tablespoons butter, softened

50 g/¼ cup soft brown sugar

½ teaspoon bicarbonate of soda/baking soda

1 teaspoon ground ginger

½ teaspoon mixed spice/apple pie spice

2 tablespoons honey

1 egg yolk

300 g/10 oz. coloured boiled sweets/hard candies, crushed

a cookie cutter

2 baking sheets lined with baking parchment

MAKES 12–15

Preheat the oven to 180°C (350°F) Gas 4.

Put the flour into a large mixing bowl and rub in the butter until it resembles fine breadcrumbs. Add the sugar and mix well. Stir in the bicarbonate of soda/baking soda, ground ginger and mixed spice/apple pie spice. Add the honey and egg yolk and bring the mixture together to form a smooth dough.

On a clean, lightly floured work surface, roll the dough out into a large rectangle with a thickness of about 3 mm/⅛ in. Cut out cookies using the cutter of your choice, arrange the cookies on the prepared baking sheets and then cut out shapes from the centre of each cookie (this is an easier way to do it than trying to move the cookie when it has the centre cut out). Bring the dough cut out of the centre together with any scraps and roll out again to cut as many cookies out of the dough as possible.

Fill the centre of each cookie with some crushed boiled sweets and bake in the preheated oven for about 10 minutes, until the cookies are golden and firm and the boiled sweets have melted and formed a stained glass window effect.

Remove from the oven and leave for 10 minutes or so to cool, before transferring to a wire rack to cool completely. Leave to set, store between layers of baking parchment in an airtight container or cookie jar and eat within 3 days. Or, if using as a decoration for your Christmas tree, thread a festive string through the top and hang up – but better not to eat them once they've been hung for a while.

PEPPARKAKOR

70 g/5 tablespoons butter

90 g/scant $\frac{1}{2}$ cup dark muscovado sugar

1 tablespoon thick gutsy honey

250 g/2 cups plain/all-purpose flour

$\frac{1}{2}$ teaspoon bicarbonate of soda/ baking soda

2 teaspoons ground ginger

1 teaspoons ground cinnamon

1 teaspoon mixed spice/apple pie spice

a pinch of salt

2 tablespoons milk

To decorate

280 g/2$\frac{1}{2}$ cups icing/ confectioners' sugar

1 egg white, lightly beaten

1–2 star-shaped cookie cutters

2 baking sheets lined with baking parchment

a piping/pastry bag fitted with a plain writing nozzle/tip

MAKES ABOUT 20

These lovely spiced biscuits are popular in Scandinavian countries at Christmas time and can be cut into any Christmassy shape you prefer and decorated to look really special. It's always really nice to have a festive treat to hand when visitors call. They're also good to hang on the Christmas tree, just make sure you poke holes in the tops before baking.

Preheat the oven to 180°C (350°F) Gas 4.

Put the butter, dark muscovado sugar and honey into a saucepan and heat gently until the butter is melted and the sugar has dissolved. Leave to cool a little.

Put the flour, bicarbonate of soda/baking soda, spices and salt into a large mixing bowl. Pour over the melted butter mixture and add the milk. Bring everything together to form a smooth dough.

On a clean, lightly floured work surface, roll the dough out into a large rectangle with a thickness of about 3 mm/$\frac{1}{8}$ in. Cut out cookies using the cutters of your choice. Bring the trimmed dough together and roll out again to cut as many cookies out of the dough as possible. Arrange the cookies on the prepared baking sheets, leaving a little space for spreading between each one.

Bake in the preheated oven for 8–10 minutes, until firm.

Leave to cool on the baking sheets for 5 minutes or so, before transferring to a wire rack to cool completely.

In the meantime, put the icing/confectioners' sugar into a bowl and beat in the egg white, until you have a thick, smooth icing. Spoon the mixture into the piping/pastry bag and decorate the biscuits as you wish!

Leave to set, store between layers of baking parchment in an airtight container or cookie jar and eat within 3 days.

LEBKUCHEN

175 g/³/₄ cup fairly gutsy honey

180 g/1 scant cup dark
   muscovado sugar

2 tablespoons black treacle/dark
   molasses

30 g/2 tablespoons butter

375 g/3 cups plain/all-purpose
   flour

a pinch of salt

¹/₂ teaspoon bicarbonate of soda/
   baking soda

2 teaspoons ground cinnamon

2 teaspoons ground mixed spice/
   apple pie (or other favourite
   spice mix)

grated zest of 1 lemon

grated zest of 1 orange

1 large egg, beaten

Glaze

100 ml/¹/₂ cup caster/granulated
   sugar

2 tablespoons freshly squeezed
   lemon juice

2 tablespoons freshly squeezed
   orange juice

40 g/¹/₃ cup icing/confectioners'
   sugar

1–2 cookie cutters

*2 baking sheets lined with
   baking parchment*

MAKES ABOUT 30

Fans of all things spicy and fragrant will love these German-style festive cookies. They have Christmas written all over them, but I love to eat them at other times of the year too, varying the cookie cutter that I use. I love to use the ready-made spice mix you can buy for pain d'épices, the gorgeous French gingerbread loaf so popular in many European countries. It has a mixture of cinnamon, cloves, aniseed, coriander and star anise. You can however substitute your own favourite spice mix (not to be confused with allspice, which is something entirely different).

Preheat the oven to 180°C (350°F) Gas 4.

Melt the honey, sugar, black treacle/molasses and butter in a small saucepan set over a low heat. Set aside to cool.

In a large mixing bowl, mix the flour, salt, bicarbonate of soda/baking soda, spices and orange and lemon zests together.

Pour the honey mixture into the dry ingredients and add the egg. Mix everything really well and bring it together to form a soft dough.

Roll the dough out between two sheets of baking parchment to a thickness of roughly 2.5 mm/¹/₁₆ in. and cut out shapes using a cookie cutter. Bring the trimmed dough together and roll out again to cut as many cookies out of the dough as possible. Arrange the cookies on the prepared baking sheets, leaving a little space for spreading between each one.

Bake in the preheated oven for 8–10 minutes, until risen and firm.

In the meantime, make the glaze. Put the caster/granulated sugar, 100 ml/ 6 tablespoons water and both juices into a small saucepan and cook over a medium heat until the sugar has melted. Bubble the mixture for 4–5 minutes, until it has thickened and become syrupy. Leave to cool a little and stir in the icing/confectioners' sugar.

Remove the biscuits from the oven and glaze whilst still hot. Cool on a wire rack and leave to set. Store between layers of baking parchment in an airtight container or cookie jar and eat within 3 days.

POLVORONES

You don't need to have a Mexican wedding planned in order to make these gorgeous cinnamon sugar-dusted pecan cookies. As well as weddings, they're quite popular as a Christmas cookie, but in fact they're so irresistible to eat and easy to make that they're bound to become a favourite for any time of the year.

120 g/1 stick butter

150 g/1 cup plus 2^1/$_2$ tablespoons plain/all-purpose flour

50 g/^{1}/$_2$ cup icing/confectioners' sugar

a pinch of salt

100 g/^{2}/$_3$ cup pecan nuts, very finely chopped

Cinnamon sugar

100 g/1 cup icing/confectioners' sugar

1 teaspoon ground cinnamon

2 baking sheets lined with baking parchment

MAKES ABOUT 18–20

Preheat the oven to 180°C (350°F) Gas 4.

Put the butter, flour, icing/confectioners' sugar and salt together in a large mixing bowl and work together until you have a smooth dough. Add the finely chopped pecans and knead gently until they are fully and evenly incorporated.

Form the mixture into balls the size of walnuts and arrange on the prepared baking sheets.

Bake in the preheated oven for 10–12 minutes, until firm and golden.

Remove from the oven and leave to cool for 5 minutes or so, before transferring to a wire rack to cool completely.

While the cookies are cooling, mix the icing/confectioners' sugar and cinnamon together. Dust the cooled cookies quite heavily with the cinnamon sugar to serve or store in an airtight container or cookie jar and eat within 5 days.

SOMETHING SPECIAL

CANDIED PINEAPPLE & STEM GINGER FLORENTINES

These delicious, delicate little Florentines make great petit fours – although they're equally nice with a morning brew. If I'm in a hurry, I serve them with a simple zigzag of chocolate drizzled over the top to decorate. If I want something a little more luxurious, I coat the bases with really good-quality dark/bittersweet chocolate, too.

60 g/$^1/_2$ stick butter

60 g/$^1/_3$ cup caster/granulated sugar

1 tablespoon honey

a pinch of salt

50 g/$^1/_3$ cup plus 1 tablespoon plain/all-purpose flour

50 g/$^1/_3$ cup flaked/slivered almonds

50 g/$^1/_3$ cup candied pineapple, chopped

50 g/1$^1/_2$ oz. stem ginger, chopped

1 tablespoon double/heavy cream

200 g/6$^1/_2$ oz. dark/bittersweet chocolate, broken into pieces (optional)

50 g/1$^1/_2$ oz. white chocolate

2 baking sheets lined with baking parchment

MAKES ABOUT 15

Preheat the oven to 180°C (350°F) Gas 4.

Melt the butter, sugar and honey together in a small saucepan set over a low heat. Remove from the heat and leave to cool slightly. Stir in the all the remaining ingredients, except the chocolate.

Drop teaspoonfuls of the mixture onto the prepared baking sheets, leaving a little space for spreading between each one.

Bake in the preheated oven for 8–10 minutes, until golden.

Remove from the oven, leave to cool slightly and then transfer to a wire rack.

Put the dark/bittersweet chocolate (if using) and white chocolate, into separate heatproof bowls and set each over a saucepan of barely simmering water to melt. Spread the smoother side of each Florentine with dark/bittersweet chocolate and leave to set. Decorate the reverse side of each Florentine with a zigzag of melted white chocolate.

Store in an airtight container in a cool place (but not the fridge), so the chocolate doesn't melt, and eat within 3 days.

CHOCOLATE-STUFFED SABLÉS

These pretty biscuits have a lovely chocolate centre encased inside buttery, crisp cookie. Getting the chocolate on the inside may seem complicated at first glance, but I promise it's easy peasy. I think you'll be chuffed to bits to add these to your cookie repertoire and share them with friends and family, I know I was!

150 g/1 cup plus
  2¹/₂ tablespoons plain/
  all-purpose flour

100 g/²/₃ cup ground almonds

100 g/¹/₂ cup caster/granulated
  sugar

150 g/1 stick plus 2 tablespoons
  butter, softened

1 egg yolk

120 g/4 oz. dark/bittersweet
  chocolate, broken into small
  pieces

a round cookie cutter

*a baking sheet lined with baking
  parchment*

MAKES ABOUT 15

Preheat the oven to 180°C (350°F) Gas 4.

Put the flour, ground almonds and sugar into a large mixing bowl and rub in the butter. Add the egg yolk and bring the mixture together to form a smooth dough.

On a clean, lightly floured work surface, roll the dough out into a large rectangle with a thickness of about 3 mm/¹/₈ in. Cut out circles about 3 cm/1¹/₄ in. wide using a round cookie cutter. Bring the trimmed dough together and roll out again to cut as many cookies out of the dough as possible.

Place a piece of chocolate in the centre of half of the circles. Top each circle with another and gently pinch the edges to seal.

Arrange the cookies on the prepared baking sheet, leaving a little space for spreading between each one, and bake in the preheated oven for about 10 minutes, until firm and golden.

Leave to cool on the baking sheet for 10–15 minutes, before transferring to a wire rack to cool completely.

Melt any leftover chocolate in a heatproof bowl set over a pan of barely simmering water and decorate the top of each cookie with zigzags of chocolate. Store in an airtight container or cookie jar and eat within 5 days.

left: orange tuiles
right: vanilla tuiles

ORANGE TUILES

These are exquisite little tuiles that make the whole kitchen smell wonderful as they are cooking. Served alongside any creamy dessert, they will add a really special something. Try to choose quite a delicate honey that won't mask the flavour of the orange zest and make sure you store them in an airtight container as soon as they are cold or they will lose their crisp texture.

50 g/3¹/₂ tablespoons butter

50 g/¹/₄ cup caster/granulated sugar

50 g/3 tablespoons clear honey

50 g/¹/₃ cup plus 1 tablespoon plain/all-purpose flour

a pinch of salt

grated zest of 1 large orange

1 tablespoon orange juice

2 baking sheets lined with baking parchment

MAKES ABOUT 12

Preheat the oven to 180°C (350°F) Gas 4.

Put the butter, sugar and honey together in a small saucepan and set over gentle heat until the butter has melted and the sugar has dissolved. Remove the pan from the heat and stir in the flour, salt and orange zest, then the orange juice. Leave the mixture to cool.

Drop tablespoons of the mixture onto the prepared baking sheets, leaving plenty of space for spreading between each one.

Bake (one sheet at a time) in the preheated oven for 8–10 minutes, until the tuiles are golden.

Remove from the oven and leave to cool on the baking sheets for a couple of minutes. With a narrow metal spatula or palette knife, carefully lift each cookie from the baking sheet and drape over a rolling pin to form a tuile. If the tuiles harden too much to shape, simply return to the oven for a minute or so to soften, cool a little and try again.

Leave until completely cold, store in an airtight container or cookie jar and eat within 2 days.

VANILLA TUILES

These lovely, crispy, light-as-air tuiles are absolutely gorgeous served with ice cream. When I have time, I cut a template with four oval shapes from the lid of a disposable foil container. It makes shaping them an absolute doddle because it's easy just to scrape the mixture over the top of each cut out shape. Don't panic if you don't fancy that idea, free form works well too – just make sure to get the mixture nice and thin and even. If the tuile starts to go crisp before you've had chance to shape it, just return it to the oven for 30 seconds or so until warm and pliable again.

40 g/3 tablespoons butter, softened

50 g/^{1}/$_3$ cup icing/confectioners' sugar

1 egg white

40 g/^{1}/$_3$ cup plain/all-purpose flour

seeds from 1 vanilla pod/bean (or ^{1}/$_4$ teaspoon vanilla paste)

a baking sheet lined with baking parchment

MAKES 8–10

Preheat the oven to 160°C (300°F) Gas 2.

Beat the butter, sugar and egg white together in a large mixing bowl until smooth. Add the flour and vanilla, and beat again. Spread the mixture onto the prepared baking sheet in small oval shapes or circles (using a template you have made, if preferred), leaving plenty of space for spreading between each one.

Bake (one sheet at a time) in the preheated oven for 4–5 minutes, until golden.

Remove from the oven. Let cool for a few seconds then with a narrow metal spatula, carefully lift each cookie from the baking sheet and drape over a rolling pin to form a tuile.

Leave until completely cold, store in an airtight container or cookie jar and eat within 2 days.

PINK PEPPERCORN LACE TUILES

This is a variation on the Black & white sesame seed tuile recipe (page 143) and is every bit as special, just slightly different. Amazing with coconut ice cream.

75 g/³/₄ cup icing/confectioners' sugar

25 g/3 tablespoons plain/all-purpose flour

50 g/3¹/₂ tablespoons butter, melted and cooled

1 tablespoon dried pink peppercorns, crushed

2 baking sheets lined with baking parchment

MAKES ABOUT 15

Preheat the oven to 180°C (350°F) Gas 4.

Mix the icing/confectioners' sugar together with 20 ml/4 teaspoons cold water in a large mixing bowl. Stir in the flour and melted butter. Stir through the crushed pink peppercorns.

Drop teaspoonfuls of the mixture onto the prepared baking sheets, leaving plenty of space for spreading between each one.

Bake (one sheet at a time) in the preheated oven for 5–6 minutes, until golden.

Remove from the oven and leave to cool on the baking sheets for a couple of minutes. With a narrow metal spatula or palette knife, carefully lift each cookie from the baking sheet and drape over a rolling pin to form a tuile. If the tuiles harden too much to shape, simply return to the oven for a minute or so to soften, cool a little and try again.

Leave until completely cold, store in an airtight container or cookie jar and eat within 2 days.

BLACK & WHITE SESAME SEED TUILES

I have this recipe on a fairly battered piece of paper in my little stash of recipes I use lots, but I think the original came from Gordon Ramsay and involved black pepper. I use white and black sesame seeds because they taste fab and look great. It's an easy peasy recipe and the tuiles spread quite a bit into funky shapes. Here I've suggested draping them over a rolling pin, but I do all sort of different things with them to make some quite groovy creations – you should do the same!

75 g/³/₄ cup icing/confectioners'
  sugar

25 g/1¹/₂ tablespoons plain/
  all-purpose flour

50 g/3¹/₂ tablespoons butter,
  melted and cooled

30 g/¹/₄ cup white sesame seeds

2 tablespoons black sesame
  seeds

*2 baking sheets lined with
  baking parchment*

MAKES ABOUT 15

Preheat the oven to 180°C (350°F) Gas 4.

Mix the sugar together with 1 teaspoon cold water in a large mixing bowl. Stir in the flour and melted butter. Add the white and black sesame seeds and stir until everything is combined.

Drop teaspoonfuls of the mixture onto the prepared baking sheets, leaving plenty of space for spreading between each one.

Bake (one sheet at a time) in the preheated oven for 5–6 minutes, until golden.

Remove from the oven and leave to cool on the baking sheets for a couple of minutes. With a narrow metal spatula or palette knife, carefully lift each cookie from the baking sheet and drape over a rolling pin to form a tuile. If the tuiles harden too much to shape, simply return to the oven for a minute or so to soften, cool a little and try again.

Leave until completely cold, store in an airtight container or cookie jar and eat within 2 days.

CHOCOLATE ORANGE PILLOWS

These cookies are based on a recipe given to me by a chef I once worked with which seemed a little complicated at first, but I've had a little tinker and now they're a doddle to make – and an absolute delight to eat. The original recipe calls for the addition of orange liqueur (and by all means add a tablespoon if you happen to have some in the cupboard), but I use the lovely Lindt chocolate that has a gorgeous orange flavour, and the recipe works really well.

200 g/6$\frac{1}{2}$ oz. dark/bittersweet chocolate

200 g/6$\frac{1}{2}$ oz. orange flavoured chocolate (I use Lindt)

50 g/3$\frac{1}{2}$ tablespoons butter

3 eggs

100 g/$\frac{2}{3}$ cup ground almonds

100 g/$\frac{3}{4}$ cup plain/all-purpose flour

100 g/1 cup icing/confectioners' sugar

1 teaspoon baking powder

grated zest of 2 oranges

Coating

50 g/$\frac{1}{2}$ cup icing/confectioners' sugar

50 g/$\frac{1}{4}$ cup caster/granulated sugar

2 baking sheets lined with baking parchment

MAKES 25–30

Preheat the oven to 180°C (350°F) Gas 4.

Melt all the chocolate and butter together in a large mixing bowl set over a saucepan of barely simmering water (or microwave on full power for a minute or so, stirring half way through). Leave to cool a little and then beat in the eggs.

Add the ground almonds, flour, icing/confectioners' sugar and baking powder and beat until well mixed. Add the orange zest and stir until evenly mixed. Pop the mixture in the fridge for 30 minutes or so to firm up.

Put the icing/confectioners' sugar and caster/granulated sugar for coating in separate wide, shallow dishes and set aside.

Form the dough into balls the size of walnuts, then roll each ball in the icing/confectioners' sugar, then in the caster/granulated sugar, and then back in the icing/confectioners' sugar again. Arrange the cookie balls on the prepared baking sheets, leaving a little space for spreading between each one.

Bake in the preheated oven for about 10 minutes, until the cookies are firm on the outside but still soft in the centre.

Leave to cool slightly on the baking sheets, before transferring to a wire rack to cool completely. Store in an airtight container or cookie jar and eat within 3 days.

CHOCOLATE GANACHE WHIRLS

These look lovely and taste lovely and make a very special offering alongside a cup of tea or coffee, but can also be made slightly smaller and served as petit fours.

160 g/1 stick plus 3 tablespoons butter, softened

80 g/6$\frac{1}{2}$ tablespoons Demerara/turbinado sugar

180 g/1$\frac{1}{3}$ cups plain/all-purpose flour

10 g/1 heaping tablespoon unsweetened cocoa powder

a pinch of salt

1 tablespoon milk

caster/superfine sugar, for dusting

Filling

150 ml/$\frac{2}{3}$ cup double heavy cream

150 g/5 oz. dark/bittersweet chocolate, broken into pieces

10 g/2 teaspoons butter, softened

a pinch of salt

a piping/pastry bag fitted with a large star nozzle/tip

2 baking sheets lined with baking parchment

MAKES ABOUT 12

Preheat the oven to 180°C (350°F) Gas 4.

Beat the butter and sugar together in a large mixing bowl until light and fluffy. Add the cocoa powder, flour and salt. Stir in the milk and bring the mixture together to form a soft dough.

Spoon the dough into the piping/pastry bag and pipe rosette shapes onto the prepared baking sheets, leaving a little space for spreading between each one.

Bake in the preheated oven for 8–10 minutes, until firm.

Leave to cool on the baking sheets for 5 minutes or so, before transferring to a wire rack to cool completely.

In the meantime, make the ganache. Pour the cream into a saucepan set over a low heat and warm gently. Add the chocolate and stir until it has completely melted. Leave until almost cold and then beat in the butter and salt.

When the ganache is completely cold, sandwich the cookies together and dust lightly with caster/superfine sugar to serve or store in an airtight container or cookie jar and eat within 3 days.

LANGUES DE CHAT

Langues de chat biscuits take their name from the French word for 'cat's tongues', because these crisp little biscuits look just like cat's tongues when they're baked. I like to serve them alongside ice cream and creamy desserts, but you can make them slightly larger and sandwich them together with a little cream then dust them with icing/confectioners' sugar, or even make mini ice cream sandwiches in the summer. Try adding the seeds from a vanilla pod/bean or some finely grated orange zest to ring the changes.

65 g/4$\frac{1}{2}$ tablespoons butter, softened

40 g/$\frac{1}{4}$ cup icing/confectioners' sugar

1 egg

65 g/$\frac{1}{2}$ cup plain/all-purpose flour

seeds from 1 vanilla pod/bean (or finely grated zest 1 medium orange)

a baking sheet lined with baking parchment

a piping/pastry bag fitted with a 1 cm/$\frac{3}{8}$ in. plain nozzle/tip

MAKES ABOUT 20

Preheat the oven to 180°C (350°F) Gas 4.

Cream the butter and icing/confectioners' sugar together in a large mixing bowl until smooth. Beat in the egg, and then add the flour and the vanilla. Beat until smooth.

Spoon the dough into the piping/pastry bag and pipe lines about 4–5 cm/ 1$\frac{1}{2}$–2 in. long onto the baking sheet, leaving a little space for spreading between each one.

Bake in the preheated oven for about 5–6 minutes, until golden and firm.

Leave to cool slightly on the baking sheet, before transferring to a wire rack to cool completely. Store in an airtight container or cookie jar and eat within 2 days.

CHOCOLATE & HAZELNUT BRUNSLIS

These. Cookies. Are. Just. Delicious. And they have no butter or flour in them, so anyone on a dairy-free or gluten-free diet can enjoy them without worry. I think they could possibly be calorie-free, if eaten standing up, too. It's only my theory and I can't be trusted much on such matters, but they're cracking good cookies methinks.

100 g/3$\frac{1}{2}$ oz. dark/bittersweet chocolate (70% cocoa is best)

100 g/$\frac{2}{3}$ cup ground almonds

200 g/1$\frac{1}{3}$ cups ground hazelnuts

a pinch of salt

200 g/1 cup Demerara/turbinado sugar

1 egg, beaten

a cookie cutter

2 baking sheets lined with baking parchment

MAKES ABOUT 30

Preheat the oven to 180°C (350°F) Gas 4.

Melt the chocolate in a heatproof bowl set over a pan of barely simmering water. Set aside to cool a little.

Mix the ground almonds and ground hazelnuts together in a large mixing bowl. Add the salt and sugar. Mix in the cooled chocolate and egg. Bring the mixture together to form a soft dough.

On a clean, lightly floured work surface, roll the dough out into a large rectangle with a thickness of about 3 mm/$\frac{1}{8}$ in. Stamp out shapes using your favourite cookie cutter. Bring the trimmed dough together and roll out again to cut as many cookies out of the dough as possible.

Arrange the cookies on the prepared baking sheets and bake in the preheated oven for about 10 minutes or so, until firm.

Leave on the baking sheets for 10 minutes or so, to cool, before transferring to a wire rack until to cool completely. Store in an airtight container or cookie jar and eat within 5 days.

PARISIAN MACARONS

There's no doubt about it, the first time or two you make macarons, you may find them a bit fiddly, but persevere and you'll be knocking them up in next to no time and impressing everyone with your new-found pâtisserie skills. Just remember that cutting corners won't do you any favours at all. Make sure you whizz the ground almonds and icing/confectioners' sugar together until fine, and don't skimp on the standing time either. It's the standing time that gives these French treats their distinctive bases or 'legs' as they're known! Drawing templates for the macarons on the baking parchment means that they will all come out the same size and look much prettier when finished.

110 g/1 cup icing/confectioners'
   sugar

80 g/¹/₂ cup ground almonds

2 large egg whites

a pinch of salt

45 g/¹/₄ cup caster/superfine
   sugar

pink food colouring gel

good-quality raspberry jam/jelly,
   to serve

*2 baking sheets lined with
   baking parchment, each
   marked with 4 cm/
   1 ³/₄ in. circles on the
   underside of the parchment*

*a large piping/pastry bag fitted
   with a very fine nozzle/tip*

MAKES ABOUT 8

Whizz the icing/confectioners' sugar and ground almonds together in a food processor until very fine and then push the mixture through a fine meshed sieve. Set aside.

Whisk the egg whites and salt together until stiff and glossy. Add half of the caster/superfine sugar, and beat again. Add the remaining sugar and beat again until stiff and glossy.

Carefully but thoroughly, fold the almond mixture into the egg whites, until they have been fully incorporated but the mixture is still light. Very carefully add a little pink colouring and fold in until the macarons are a uniform pink colour.

Spoon the mixture into the piping/pastry bag and pipe circles onto the parchment within the circular templates.

Tap the baking sheets firmly on the work surface two or three times, to knock out any air bubbles and leave them to stand for 30 minutes. During this time, preheat the oven to 140°C (275°F) Gas 1.

Bake in the preheated oven for about 15 minutes, until the shells are crisp and the macarons have grown little 'feet'.

Remove from the oven and leave to cool completely. Sandwich the shells together with the raspberry jam/jelly.

Store in an airtight container or cookie jar and eat within 2 days, once filled.

PISTACHIO SABLÉS

These cookies are crisp, crunchy and truly irresistible. Sumptuous rounds encased in finely crushed pistachio nuts feel really indulgent.

150 g/1 stick plus 2 tablespoons butter

230 g/1²/₃ cups icing/confectioners' sugar

a pinch of salt

seeds from 1 vanilla pod/bean

170 g/1¹/₃ cups plain/all-purpose flour

50 g/¹/₃ cup ground almonds

100 g/²/₃ cup shelled unsalted pistachios, coarsely chopped

75 g/¹/₂ cup shelled unsalted pistachios, very finely chopped

1 egg white, lightly beaten

2 baking sheets lined with baking parchment

MAKES ABOUT 30

Preheat the oven to 180°C (350°F) Gas 4.

Beat the butter and icing/confectioners' sugar together in a large mixing bowl with the salt and vanilla seeds until everything is well mixed. Add the flour and almonds and work the mixture together until it forms a smooth dough. Add the coarsely chopped pistachios and knead gently but firmly, until they are incorporated evenly.

Form the mixture into two sausage shaped logs, about 2.5 cm/1 in. in diameter and wrap in clingfilm/plastic wrap, using the clingfilm/plastic wrap to help roll the dough evenly. Refrigerate for 30 minutes or so.

Scatter the finely chopped pistachios evenly over a clean work surface. Unwrap the dough and brush with the beaten egg white. Roll in the pistachio mixture until they have a fine, even layer of pistachios around the edge. Cut into slices about 1 cm/³/₈ in. thick and lay the slices on the prepared baking sheets, leaving a little space for spreading between each one.

Bake in the preheated oven for 10–12 minutes, until golden and firm.

Remove from the oven and leave to cool on a wire rack. Store in an airtight container or cookie jar and eat within 1 week.

ICED GEMS

These are for anyone who remembers the tiny little biscuits topped with swirls of crunchy, multi-coloured icing – the icing won't set as teeth-breakingly hard as the store-bought version, but that's no bad thing in my opinion! I think these are just great fun for children's parties!

180 g/1 1/3 cups plain/all-purpose flour

120 g/2/3 cup caster/granulated sugar

120 g/1 stick butter

1 egg, separated

Frosting

320 g/2 1/2 cups icing/confectioners' sugar

food colouring gels

a very small cookie cutter

2 baking sheets lined with baking parchment

2–3 piping/pastry bags with a star nozzles/tips

MAKES OVER 100

Preheat the oven to 180°C (350°F) Gas 4.

Put the flour into a large mixing bowl and stir in the sugar. Rub in the butter until the mixture resembles fine breadcrumbs. Add the egg yolk and draw the mixture together to form a smooth, soft dough.

On a clean, lightly floured work surface, roll the dough out into a large rectangle with a thickness of about 3 mm/1/8 in. Cut out tiny circles using the cookie cutter or the end of a piping/pastry nozzle/tip. Bring the trimmed dough together and roll out again to cut as many cookies out of the dough as possible. Arrange the circles on the prepared baking sheets.

Bake in the preheated oven for about 4 minutes, until golden and firm.

Leave to cool on the baking sheet.

Meanwhile, whisk the egg white until light and add the icing/confectioners' sugar. Mix until very thick and smooth. Divide the mixture into two or three batches and colour each with a little colouring gel.

Spoon the icing into the piping/pastry bags and pipe a little rosette on the top of each cookie. Leave to dry for a couple of hours before serving or store between layers of baking parchment in an airtight container or cookie jar and eat within 3 days.

FORTUNE COOKIES

Perfect to serve at the end of a homemade Chinese dinner – or great fun at parties – these cookies take a little bit of patience to get the messages sealed inside, but are well worth persevering with. They might even bring you a little good luck.

50 g/3^1/$_2$ tablespoons butter

50 g/^{1}/$_2$ cup icing/confectioners' sugar

1 egg white

^{1}/$_2$ teaspoon sesame oil

40 g/^{1}/$_3$ cup plain/all-purpose flour

2 baking sheets lined with baking parchment

small pieces of paper with various 'fortunes' written on them

MAKES 8–10

Preheat the oven to 180°C (350°F) Gas 4.

Beat the butter and sugar together in a large mixing bowl until smooth and light. Beat in the egg white and sesame oil until fully incorporated. Add the flour and stir until everything is well combined.

Spread small circles of the mixture onto the prepared baking sheets and bake in the preheated for about 6 minutes, until very light golden and firm.

Remove the cookies from the oven and let them firm up for a minute.

With a narrow metal spatula or palette knife, carefully lift each cookie from the baking sheet, pop the folded fortune in the centre and immediately fold the cookie in half, pinching the edges together. Pull the cookie around to make the traditional fortune cookie shape and leave to cool. If the cookies harden too much to shape, simply return to the oven for a minute or so to soften, cool a little and try again.

Store in an airtight container or cookie jar and eat within 2 days.

CUSTARD CREAMS

Custard powder/vanilla pudding mix is the essential ingredient in these amazing little biscuits. Of course, for me, it has to be Bird's but you're allowed to substitute a store brand variety. You're even allowed to dunk them into the custard, too.

150 g/1 stick plus 2 tablespoons
  butter

75 g/2¹/₂ oz. custard powder/
  vanilla pudding mix

75 g/¹/₃ cup caster/granulated
  sugar

150 g/1 cup plus
  2¹/₂ tablespoons plain/
  all-purpose flour

Vanilla buttercream

100 g/6¹/₂ tablespoons butter,
  softened

200 g/2 cups icing/
  confectioners' sugar

1 tablespoon milk

seeds from 1 vanilla pod/bean

a pinch of salt

*a baking sheet lined with baking
  parchment*

MAKES ABOUT 15

Preheat the oven to 180°C (350°F) Gas 4.

Put the butter, custard powder/vanilla pudding mix, caster/granulated sugar and flour together in a large mixing bowl and work everything together until it forms a soft dough.

On a clean, lightly floured work surface, roll the dough out into a large rectangle with a thickness of about 3 mm/¹/₈ in. You could use a patterned rolling pin on the last roll to make little patterns on the dough. Cut into slightly elongated squares about the size of a small matchbox. Bring the trimmed dough (if there is any) together and roll out again to cut as many cookies out of the dough as possible. Prick 3 holes in the centre of each biscuit using the tines of a fork.

Arrange the cookies on the prepared baking sheets, leaving a little space for spreading between each one.

Bake in the preheated oven for about 8 minutes, until firm and light golden.

Leave for 5 minutes or so to cool, and then transfer to a wire rack until completely cold.

In the meantime, beat all the ingredients for the buttercream together in a large mixing bowl until smooth and well mixed.

Sandwich the cookies together using the buttercream and serve or store in an airtight container or cookie jar and eat within 3 days.

BOURBON BISCUITS

Bourbons were one of my favourites as a child and they're easier to make and more fun than you might think. Originally from Bournville in England, they were named after the chocolate-producing town and the inventor's home town, Bonn in Germany. Bour-bon.

160 g/1 stick plus 3 tablespoons butter

90 g/¹/₂ cup Demerara/turbinado sugar

10 g/1 heaping tablespoon cocoa powder

180 g/1¹/₃ cups plain/all-purpose flour

a pinch of salt

caster/superfine sugar, for dusting

Chocolate buttercream

120 g/1 stick butter

175 g/1³/₄ cups icing/ confectioners' sugar

50 g/scant ¹/₂ cup cocoa powder

1 tablespoon milk

2 baking sheets lined with baking parchment

MAKES 10

Preheat the oven to 180°C (350°F) Gas 4.

Beat the butter and sugar together in a large mixing bowl until light and fluffy. Add the cocoa powder, flour and salt and bring the mixture together to form a soft dough.

On a clean, lightly floured work surface, roll the dough out into a large rectangle with a thickness of about 3 mm/¹/₈ in. Cut into rectangles of about 3 x 5 cm/ 1¹/₄ x 2 in. Bring the trimmed dough (if there is any) together and roll out again to cut as many cookies out of the dough as possible. Prick 3 holes in the centre of each biscuit using the tines of a fork.

Arrange the cookies on the prepared baking sheets, leaving a little space for spreading between each one.

Bake in the preheated oven for 8–10 minutes, until firm.

Leave to cool for 5 minutes or so, then transfer to a wire rack to cool completely.

In the meantime, make the chocolate buttercream. Beat the butter and icing/ confectioners' sugar together in a large mixing bowl. Add the cocoa powder and milk, and beat again until everything is fully combined.

Sandwich the cookies together using the chocolate buttercream, dust with caster/superfine sugar and serve or store in an airtight container or cookie jar and eat within 3 days.

SAVOURY BITES

PARMESAN, CHILLI & MARCONA ALMOND BISCUITS

These are amazing little bite-sized biscuits to serve with drinks. Don't go too mad with the chilli flakes though – one man's mild is another man's furnace! I always have rolls of the frozen cookie dough in the freezer, which make it easy to rustle up a batch when friends call round and the wine comes out. Try to use the big, buttery Spanish Marcona almonds – they have such a special flavour.

180 g/1 $^1/_2$ sticks butter, softened

100 g/1 $^1/_3$ cups finely grated Parmesan cheese

80 g/1 cup finely grated strong Cheddar cheese

180 g/1 $^1/_3$ cups plus 1 tablespoon flour

a pinch of salt

a pinch of chilli flakes/Aleppo pepper

180 g/1 $^1/_4$ cups roasted Marcona almonds, roughly chopped

a baking sheet lined with baking parchment

MAKES ABOUT 25

Beat the butter and cheeses together in a large mixing bowl. Combine the flour, salt and chilli flakes/Aleppo pepper in a separate bowl and work into the butter mixture to form a smooth dough. Add the almonds and work again until they are evenly incorporated.

Lay a piece of clingfilm/plastic wrap on a clean work surface. Lightly dust it with flour. Divide the mixture into two or three pieces and roll into long sausage shapes, about 2.5 cm/1 in. in diameter. Wrap them tightly in the clingfilm/plastic wrap and twist the ends to seal. Refrigerate for 15 minutes or so, until the dough has firmed up a little.

Preheat the oven to 180°C (350°F) Gas 4.

Unwrap the dough and cut into 3 mm/$^1/_8$ in. thick slices.

Lay on the prepared baking sheets and bake in the preheated oven for 6–8 minutes, until golden and firm.

Cool on a wire rack, store in an airtight container or cookie jar and eat within 5 days.

OLIVE OIL, ROSEMARY & SEA SALT CRACKERS

These lovely crisp crackers are great to serve alongside dips, with cheese or soup, or just to munch when you fancy something savoury. They're fun and easy to make, and contain only store-cupboard ingredients and fresh rosemary. At a pinch, you could even use dried rosemary. Just make sure to roll them out paper thin – or you could put the dough through a pasta machine if you have one. Please make sure you use extra virgin olive oil, and not sunflower or cooking oils, as the results just won't be the same. I find it easier to weigh water, as millilitre for gram it's the same and it's often easier to use scales rather than mess about trying to line up a liquid in a measuring jug/pitcher. That way, you can just pop your bowl on the scales and add all the ingredients to the mixing bowl together.

160 g/1¼ cups plain/all-purpose flour (I use Italian 00)

½ teaspoon salt

2 teaspoons very finely chopped fresh rosemary (or 1 teaspoon dried rosemary)

40 ml/3 tablespoons extra virgin olive oil

sea salt, for sprinkling

2 baking sheets lined with baking parchment

MAKES 10–12

Preheat the oven to 180°C (350°F) Gas 4.

Mix everything together with 70 ml/5 tablespoons water in a large mixing bowl and knead until smooth.

Break off pieces the size of large walnuts and on a clean, lightly floured work surface, roll out until paper thin (if you can see your hand through the dough, that's about right). Don't worry about forming even shapes; freeform will look really funky when they're cooked.

Lay the crackers carefully on the prepared baking sheet, scatter with salt and bake in the preheated oven for about 5 minutes, until golden brown and crisp.

Remove from the oven, store in an airtight container and eat within 2 days.

MULTI SEED CRACKERS

These crackers are definitely one for seed lovers (the seeds do get stuck in your teeth a little bit, but it's worth it!) They're quite crumbly and short, but lovely spread with lashings of soft cheese. I adapted the recipe from one of Nigel Slater's (thank you, Nigel), changing the quantities a little and using extra virgin olive oil rather than butter. I use those bags of mixed seeds that contain sunflower, pumpkin, sesame, hemp and linseeds, etc., but you can substitute your own favourite seeds so long as you keep the total quantities the same. Use a good oil, don't be tempted to use a cheap oil or any other type of oil other than extra virgin, or the flavour of the crackers may be bitter or just plain tasteless and you're sure to be disappointed.

200 g/1^2/$_3$ cups spelt flour
a decent pinch of salt
80 g/^{1}/$_3$ cup extra virgin olive oil
120 g/1 cup mixed seeds

2 baking sheets lined with baking parchment

MAKES ABOUT 16

Preheat the oven to 180°C (350°F) Gas 4.

Put the flour and salt into a large mixing bowl and add the oil and 4 tablespoons water. Bring the mixture together to form a soft dough and then knead in the seeds until they are all fully incorporated.

On a clean, lightly floured work surface, roll the dough out into a large rectangle about 4 mm/^{1}/$_8$ in. thick. Cut into squares and arrange on the prepared baking sheets, leaving a little space for spreading between each one. Bring the trimmed dough (if there is any) together and roll out again to cut as many crackers out of the dough as possible.

Bake in the preheated oven for 10–12 minutes, until firm and golden.

Leave to cool on the baking sheet, before transferring to wire racks to cool completely. Store in an airtight container and eat within 2 days.

SPELT & PUMPKIN SEED CRACKERS

Simple but really tasty, these crackers go really well with cheese and make a much nicer alternative to store-bought crackers.

100 g/³/₄ cup spelt flour

30 g/2 tablespoons butter

a pinch of salt

50 g/¹/₃ cup pumpkin seeds

2 baking sheets lined with baking parchment

MAKES 10–12

Preheat the oven to 180°C (350°F) Gas 4.

Put the flour into a large mixing bowl and rub in the butter until fully incorporated. Add the salt and pumpkin seeds and enough water so that you are able to bring the mixture together to form a soft (but not sticky) dough.

On a clean, lightly floured work surface, roll the dough out into a large rectangle with a thickness of about 3 mm/¹/₈ in. Cut into 3 cm/1 ¹/₄ in. squares. Bring the trimmed dough (if there is any) together and roll out again to cut as many crackers out of the dough as possible.

Arrange the crackers on the prepared baking sheets and bake in the preheated oven for about 10 minutes or so, until firm.

Leave on the baking sheets for 5–10 minutes, to cool, before transferring to a wire rack until to cool completely. Store in an airtight container and eat within 2 days.

CHIA SEED & CHEESE BISCUITS

These cheesy, seed speckled biscuits are a favourite of mine. Chia seeds are packed with goodness and can be found in good supermarkets and health shops.

125 g/1 stick butter, softened

125 g/1 cup plain/all-purpose flour

50 g/²/₃ cup finely grated Parmesan cheese

2 tablespoons chia seeds

a pinch of salt

a baking sheet lined with baking parchment

MAKES ABOUT 15

Preheat the oven to 180°C (350°F) Gas 4.

Put the butter, flour, cheese, chia seeds and salt into a large mixing bowl and draw everything together to form a smooth, soft dough.

Lay two pieces of clingfilm/plastic wrap on a clean work surface. Lightly dust with flour. Divide the mixture in two pieces and roll into long sausage shapes, about 2.5 cm/1 in. in diameter. Wrap them tightly in the clingfilm/plastic wrap and twist the edges to seal. Refrigerate for 15 minutes or so, until the dough has firmed up a little – and then unwrap and cut into 3 mm/¹/₈ in. slices.

Lay the slices on the prepared baking sheet and bake for 6–8 minutes, until golden and firm.

Cool on a wire rack, store in an airtight container and eat within 5 days.

ROSEMARY & PINE NUT COOKIES

I love these crunchy cookies with their subtle hint of rosemary. Don't skip toasting the pine nuts though, or the flavour will be a little flat.

100 g/²/₃ cup pine nuts

120 g/1 stick butter, softened

100 g/¹/₂ cup caster/granulated sugar

a pinch of salt

1 teaspoon very finely chopped fresh rosemary

140 g/1 cup plus 1¹/₂ tablespoons plain/all-purpose flour

a baking sheet lined with parchment paper

MAKES 20–25

Preheat the oven to 180°C (350°F) Gas 4.

Put the pine nuts into a large pan set over a medium heat and cook for 2–3 minutes, until toasted and golden, stirring regularly to prevent burning. Set aside to cool.

Beat the butter, sugar and salt together in a large mixing bowl until light and fluffy. Add the chopped rosemary and flour and stir until it is fully incorporated and the mixture is smooth. Add the pine nuts and stir to combine.

Drop generous teaspoons of the mixture onto the prepared baking sheet, leaving room between each for the cookies to spread.

Bake in the preheated oven for 8–10 minutes, until golden and firm.

Transfer to a wire rack – the cookies will crisp as they cool – then store in an airtight container and eat within 5 days.

BLUE CHEESE & WALNUT BISCUITS

These tasty, crumbly little treats make great pre-dinner nibbles. Freshly chopped chives make a lovely addition to the recipe, too.

90 g/6 tablespoons butter, softened

130 g/4^1/$_2$ oz. strong blue cheese, such as Roquefort

200 g/1^2/$_3$ cups plain/all-purpose flour

a pinch of salt

50 g/^{1}/$_3$ cup walnuts, chopped

2 baking sheets lined with baking parchment

MAKES ABOUT 30

Preheat the oven to 180°C (350°F) Gas 4.

Beat the butter and blue cheese together in a large mixing bowl until evenly mixed. Work in the flour and salt and bring the mixture together to form a smooth dough. Add the chopped walnuts and knead very lightly until they have all been evenly combined.

Form the mixture into two long sausage shapes and wrap both tightly in clingfilm/ plastic wrap. Refrigerate for 30 minutes or so to firm up.

Unwrap the dough and cut into slices just under 1 cm/^{3}/$_8$ in. thick. Arrange on the prepared baking sheets, leaving a little space for spreading between each one.

Bake in the preheated oven for 10–12 minutes, until crisp and golden.

Leave to cool for 5 minutes or so, before transferring to a wire rack to cool completely. Store in an airtight container and eat within 5 days.

BACON BITES

These are lovely little biscuits to serve as canapés. Chives also work well, and sometimes I use a nice strong Gruyère for something special. Occasionally I add a few chilli flakes/hot red pepper flakes and sometimes a finely chopped sun-dried tomato or two, if I have a jar open. If you can't find wafer thin pancetta, try slices of Parma ham or other prosciutto and cook in the oven until crisp in the same way as you would for the pancetta.

40 g/1 1/2 oz. very thinly sliced pancetta

50 g/3 1/2 tablespoons butter, softened

150 g/1 cup plus 2 1/2 tablespoons plain/all-purpose flour

a pinch of salt

50 g/2/3 cup finely grated Parmesan cheese

1 teaspoon very finely chopped fresh rosemary

1 egg

a baking sheet lined with baking parchment

MAKES ABOUT 20

Preheat the oven to 180°C (350°F) Gas 4.

Lay the pancetta out on a non-stick baking sheet and cook for 5 minutes, or until crisp, taking care not to let it burn. Remove from the oven, cool slightly, chop into pieces and set aside.

Rub the butter, flour and salt together in a large mixing bowl until the mixture resembles fine breadcrumbs. Stir in the Parmesan and rosemary. Add the egg and chopped pancetta and bring everything together to form a soft dough.

Roll the dough out between two sheets of baking parchment to a thickness of roughly 2.5 mm/1/16 in. and cut out shapes using a cookie cutter.

Arrange on the baking sheet and bake in the preheated oven for 8–10 minutes, until golden and firm.

Store in an airtight container and eat within 3 days.

CURRY CASHEW CRUNCH COOKIES

These crunchy little biscuits have a hint of curry, a smidgen of cumin and are speckled with curry-flavoured cashews; a sassy little combo that's great to offer round with pre-dinner drinks or just to enjoy on the sofa with a glass of wine at the weekend. Warning: curry-flavoured cashews can become addictive.

150 g/1 cup plus
   2^1/$_2$ tablespoons plain/
   all-purpose flour

^{1}/$_2$ teaspoon salt

1 tablespoon mild curry powder

1 generous teaspoon cumin
   seeds

75 g/5 tablespoons butter

1 egg, beaten

75 g/2^1/$_2$ oz. curry-flavoured
   cashew nuts

*a baking sheet lined with baking
   parchment*

MAKES ABOUT 20

Preheat the oven to 180°C (350°F) Gas 4.

Put the flour, salt and curry powder into a large mixing bowl. Stir in the cumin seeds. Rub the butter into the mixture until it resembles fine breadcrumbs, and then add the beaten egg. Draw everything together to form a smooth dough.

Eat some of the cashew nuts, but try to leave 50 g/1^1/$_2$ oz. which you should roughly chop and knead into the dough.

Roll the dough into a log shape and wrap tightly in clingfilm/plastic wrap. Refrigerate for 30 minutes or so to firm up.

Unwrap the dough and cut into slices just under 1 cm/^{3}/$_8$ in. thick. Arrange on the prepared baking sheets, leaving a little space for spreading between each one.

Bake in the preheated oven for about 10 minutes, until crisp and golden.

Leave to cool for 5 minutes or so, before transferring to a wire rack to cool completely. Store in an airtight container and eat within 5 days.

left: sun-dried tomato shortbread
right: gruyère, anchovy & fennel seed shortbread

SUN-DRIED TOMATO SHORTBREAD

It's always nice to have a little something to nibble on alongside a drink – and these moreish tomato-speckled shortbreads beat a bowl of cheese and onion crisps/chips every time! Black sesame seeds make them look especially pretty and add an extra element of flavour. They should be easy to get hold of from large supermarkets and Asian stores, but if you can't find them (or don't fancy the idea of using them), please don't worry – these shortbread still taste really special without them; I often serve a combination of both.

100 g/6^1/$_2$ tablespoons butter

100 g/1^1/$_3$ cups grated Parmesan cheese

150 g/1 cup plus 2^1/$_2$ tablespoons plain/all-purpose flour

80 g/^{1}/$_2$ cup sun-dried tomatoes, patted dry on paper towels and roughly chopped

2 egg whites, lightly beaten

40 g/^{1}/$_3$ cup black sesame seeds

2 baking sheets lined with baking parchment

MAKES ABOUT 25

Preheat the oven to 180°C (350°F) Gas 4.

Work the butter, cheese and flour together in a large mixing bowl until you have a soft, smooth dough. Gently knead the tomatoes into the dough.

Divide the mixture in half and roll the pieces into long sausage shapes, about 2.5 cm/1 in. in diameter. Wrap them tightly in clingfilm/plastic wrap and twist the ends to seal. Refrigerate for 30 minutes, to give the dough a chance to firm up.

Put the sesame seeds in a wide, shallow dish and set aside.

Unwrap the dough and brush with the beaten egg white. Roll in the sesame seeds and cut into slices about 1 cm/^{3}/$_8$ in. thick.

Lay the slices on the prepared baking sheets and bake in the preheated oven for 8–10 minutes, until golden and firm.

Cool on a wire rack, store in an airtight container and eat within 3 days.

GRUYÈRE, ANCHOVY & FENNEL SEED SHORTBREAD

These make fab little party bites – the fennel seeds make them very moreish. If you're not a fan of fennel seeds, try freshly chopped chives instead.

100 g/^{3}/$_4$ cup plain/all-purpose flour

100 g/6^1/$_2$ tablespoons butter, softened

80 g/^{3}/$_4$ cup finely grated Gruyère (mature, if possible)

6 anchovies, rinsed, dried and finely chopped

1 teaspoon fennel seeds

a baking sheet lined with baking parchment

MAKES ABOUT 20

Preheat the oven to 180°C (350°F) Gas 4.

Put all the ingredients into a large mixing bowl and work everything together to form a soft dough.

Lay two pieces of clingfilm/plastic wrap on a clean work surface. Lightly dust with flour. Divide the mixture in two and roll into long sausage shapes, about 3 cm/1 ^{1}/$_4$ in. in diameter. Wrap them tightly in the clingfilm/plastic wrap and twist the edges to seal. Refrigerate for 15 minutes or so, until the dough has firmed up a little – and then cut into 3 mm/^{1}/$_8$ in. slices.

Lay the slices the prepared baking sheet and bake in the preheated oven for 6–8 minutes, until golden and firm.

Cool on a wire rack, store in an airtight container and eat within 3 days.

CHEESY FEET BISCUITS

These savoury biscuits may sound cheeky, but they really are crisp, cheesy and delicious. If you're not keen on them being foot shaped, then you can simply form the dough into logs and cut into slices, or cut out different shapes using other cutters. Whatever you choose to do, I think you'll agree these are a doddle to make and a delight to eat.

100 g/³/₄ cup plain/all-purpose flour

100 g/6¹/₂ tablespoons butter

100 g/1¹/₃ cups grated Parmesan cheese

100 g/1¹/₃ cups grated strong Cheddar cheese

a pinch of salt

a pinch of cayenne pepper (optional)

a foot-shaped cookie cutter

a baking sheet lined with baking parchment

MAKES ABOUT 12

Preheat the oven to 180°C (350°F) Gas 4.

Put all the ingredients together in a large mixing bowl and mix until evenly combined. Draw the mixture together to form a soft dough. Wrap the dough in clingfilm/plastic wrap and chill for about 1 hour.

On a clean, lightly floured work surface, roll the dough out into a large rectangle about 4 mm/¹/₈ in. thick. Cut out feet with the cutter and arrange on the prepared baking sheets, leaving a little space for spreading between each one. Bring the trimmed dough together and roll out again to cut as many feet out of the dough as possible.

Bake in the preheated oven for 18–20 minutes, until golden and firm.

Leave to cool for 5 minutes or so and then transfer to a wire rack to cool completely. Store in an airtight container and eat within 3 days.

CHILLI & SAFFRON BISCOTTI

These unusual savoury biscotti are great to serve with cheese as an alternative to crackers and make a really special accompaniment to soups, dips and all manner of savoury dishes. You could serve them with pre-dinner drinks, too.

a good pinch of saffron threads

250 g/2 cups plain/all-purpose flour

½ teaspoon salt

1 teaspoon chilli flakes/hot red pepper flakes

2 eggs

100 g/⅔ cup finely chopped walnuts

2 baking sheets lined with baking parchment

MAKES ABOUT 25

Soak the saffron threads in 1 tablespoon of water for about 30 minutes.

Preheat the oven to 180°C (350°F) Gas 4.

Mix the flour, salt and chilli flakes/hot red pepper flakes together in a large mixing bowl, and then add the eggs and the soaked saffron and its water. Bring the mixture together to form a smooth dough and knead gently for a minute or so. Add the walnuts and knead gently until they are fully incorporated.

Form the mixture into two long logs and place them on one of the prepared baking sheets. Bake in the preheated oven for 25–30 minutes, until firm and golden. Remove from the oven and leave to cool, but keep the heat on.

Cut the logs into slices about 1 cm/³⁄₈ in. thick and arrange on both baking sheets.

Bake in the still-warm oven for 10 minutes, until firm and golden.

Leave to cool on the baking sheets for 5 minutes or so, before transferring to a wire rack to cool completely. Store in an airtight container and eat within 5 days.

INDEX

ACKNOWLEDGEMENTS

With huge thanks to the wonderful team at RPS... Maria, Megan, Gordana, Leslie, Cindy, Hilary and of course Julia Charles for creating a book of which I am incredibly proud.

A big shout out to my editor, Stephanie Milner, for her patience, enthusiasm and encouragement, and for always being there to iron out the little wrinkles!

Thank you to Annie Rigg for the gorgeous food styling, to Jo Harris for the most perfect props, and to Kate Whitaker for the beautiful photography.

And lastly, but by no means least, thank you to my wonderful family for their constant love, support and inspiration, through everything, xxx.

SUPPLIERS

UK

Amazon
www.amazon.co.uk

Cakes, Cookies & Crafts
www.cakescookiesandcraftsshop.co.uk

Cookie Cutter Shop
www.cookiecuttershop.co.uk

The Craft Company
www.craftcompany.co.uk

Hobbycraft
www.hobbycraft.co.uk

Lakeland
www.lakeland.co.uk

USA

Amazon
www.amazon.com

CookieCutter.com
www.cookiecutter.com

The Cookie Cutter Company
www.cookiecuttercompany.com

The Copper Cookie Cutter Store
www.thecoppercookiecutterstore.com

J B Cookie Cutters
www.jbcookiecutters.com

La Cuisine
www.lacuisineus.com

Michaels
www.michaels.com

Wilton
www.wilton.com

Australia

Bisk-Art
www.biskart.com.au

Cakes Around Town
www.cakesaroundtown.com.au

Cookie Cutter Shop
www.cookiecuttershop.com.au